First published in 2018
by Steven John Burt

Book ISBN 978-0-9570538-6-1
Ebook ASIN B07G88V4S9

Published by Chapel Rank Publications

Other titles by the same author.

Growing up in Lederhosen
Boys to Men

In writing this book I called upon many ex-16 Squadron Sappers to
verify events names and places. I thank you all for your input,
photos and memories.

About the author

Steven grew up in a small West Country village during the sixties.

With a German mum and English dad life was at times confusing but not boring.

Although well-mannered and polite Steven was not the best behaved kid on the block and soon began to flash on the radar of the local village policeman. No matter how harsh the punishment misbehaviour persisted and school results plummeted; parents despaired.

John and Elsa's rising concerns were brought to a halt when their now fourteen year old wayward son came home from school one evening and announced he was leaving home to become a boy soldier in the Royal Engineers.

From that moment life changed; two years as a Junior Leader Royal Engineer stationed at Dover followed by four years in Germany defending the free west from the Soviet hordes posed in readiness behind the Iron Curtain and active service tours on the streets of Northern Ireland changed Steve from boy to man.

The years that followed his time in the Army were interesting and exciting with jobs in the oil industry and the world of International marine tourism, the latter taking him all over the world through numerous contracts and adventures.

Steven eventually married in 2010 and settled in Norfolk where he works in a variety of management roles; now approaching retirement he hopes to fulfil a final ambition to live a few years in the country of his mother's birth, which he dearly loves, Germany and eventually settle back in West Wiltshire.

Chapters

British Army of the Rhine

The second British Army of the Rhine (1BR Corp) was formed on 25 August 1945 from 21st Army Group. Its original function was to control the Corps districts which were running the military government of the British zone of occupied Germany.

After the assumption of government by civilians, BAOR became the command formation for the troops in Germany only, rather than being responsible for administration as well.

As the potential threat of Soviet invasion across the north German plain into West Germany increased, the role of BAOR changed; it became more responsible for the defence of West Germany rather than a force of occupation. It became the primary formation controlling the British contribution to NATO.

Its primary combat formation was British I Corps.

From 1952 the commander-in-chief of BAOR was (in the event of a general war with the Soviet Union and the Warsaw Pact) the commander of NATO's Northern Army Group (NORTHAG).

In 1967, the force was reduced in strength to 53,000 soldiers.

Until the fragmentation of the Soviet Bloc in the late eighties and the fall of Communism at the same time, this intervening period had been called the Cold War and the border the 'Iron Curtain'. A heavily guarded and patrolled demarcation line running the length of Europe, this was the front line. From the Baltic coastal town of Travemünde to the Czech Republic, and what was then Yugoslavia.

During this period of Cold War NATO armies waited in readiness for what every Senior Military Commander and Allied

Defence Chief considered inevitable; the surprise attack from Eastern Bloc Forces.

Our grossly outnumbered, and in some areas grossly ill equipped armies trained constantly for what would be the defence of the free west.

However BAOR was at this time armed with tactical nuclear weapons which probably went a long way to assist in securing and maintaining our freedom.

Bumping along in amber alert status the majority of the time when red alerts happened and they did occasionally; we, The Cold War front liners would leave our beds in the middle of the night and head for our harbour areas in the forests around Fulda and Warburg. But Black Alert never happened. We can be thankful it never did because outnumbered one hundred to one we were ill equipped to deal with the rolling 'Red Tide'.

The 1993 'Options for Change' defence cuts resulted in BAOR being replaced by the 25,000 strong - British Forces Germany.

Garrisons which closed at this time included Soest home of the 6th Armoured Brigade, Soltau home of the 7th Armoured Brigade and Minden home of the 11th Armoured Brigade.

My barracks - Roberts Barracks, Osnabruck were handed back to the German authorities in 2014. It has since been demolished.

We, the soldiers and airmen who served in BAOR during those years from the late forties to the end of the eighties were effectively the front line of the Cold War.

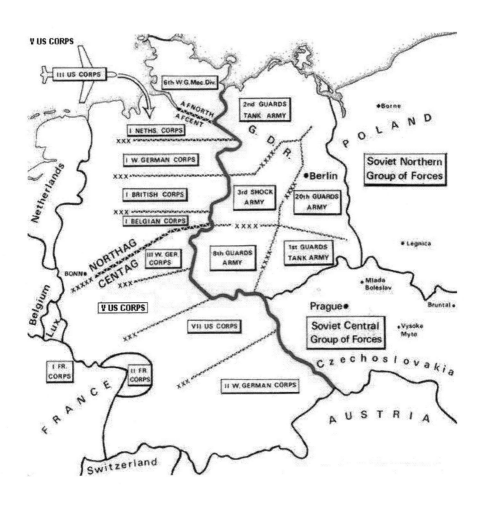

Prologue

I've just finished two years as a Junior Soldier; a Junior Leader Royal Engineer. I'm six months off my eighteenth birthday... yet on my way to Germany to join 16 Field Squadron based as part of 23 Engineer Regiment in Osnabruck. I will spend four years in Sixteen and enjoy my time here immensely. Sixteen no longer exists as a Field Squadron; it was disbanded in 1991, sad as it was one of the first Engineer Squadrons ever formed under Wellington as a survey Squadron in 1825. In fact the Squadron celebrated its 150th anniversary in 1975 while I was still there.

During my four years I found Sixteen to be a very happy Squadron and now, forty years on and in touch with many ex-Sixteeners who served before me, with me and after me. I get the same feedback. It seems it was a Squadron where Sappers enjoyed their time. I would have stayed longer with the Squadron given the opportunity to do so. I was needed (they told me) somewhere else.

The job of the Royal Engineer Field Squadron in BAOR at the time was to support the infantry battle group in preventing or slowing an Eastern Bloc invasion of the West. All Field Squadrons had their areas of operations. We all knew where we were going and what we had to do and practiced constantly our defensive role.

Our engineer tasks in front of the advancing enemy were mainly to lay mine fields and destroy bridges and roads. These were the two primary jobs that we practiced over and over again around Kassel, Warburg and to the West of the Fulda Gap an area between the Hesse-Thuringian border (the former intra-German border) and Frankfurt am Main that contains two corridors of lowlands through which Soviet tanks and their Warsaw Pact allies would have driven a surprise attack to gain a crossing of the Rhine River.

The Fulda Gap as we called it was strategically important during the Cold War. The Reds had to go through it. To the North and South the heavily forested mountainous country did not allow for tank warfare.

We spent far more time practicing our defensive role than an attacking one – destruction rather than construction; this logic I'm pretty certain was based on the fact that we, the West, wouldn't be launching an attack on the Eastern Bloc but defending under extreme pressure.

The Cold War - how we operated, trained, and waited for the day Brezhnev gave the word to his troops is a distant memory; but it should not be forgotten. I will try in this and other books to give an insight into the life of a young soldier – a Sapper, during the decade of the seventies in cold war Germany *and Ulster*.

It will be my story; it will contain bad language and a few x-rated exploits; I had contemplated keeping the more personnel escapades out of the story, but then it wouldn't be a true reflection of what I and others got up to. So with the agreement of my long suffering wife I've not skimped on the detail.

Most of us were pretty gung-ho and care-free, I'm sure this story will resonate with many.

Roberts Barracks original name Winkelhausen Kaserne.

First in use by German armed forces in 1935.
This aerial photograph is one of the more recent. The Church and swimming pool are gone; also the refuelling point. The large open parking area and wash-down point that fronted 16 Squadron garages has been built over; however, apart from those major changes the barrack is very much as it was during my time there during the mid-seventies.
The barrack was demolished in 2016.

Part 1
Welcome to 16 Squadron - Pre-Operation Banner

Leaving Blighty

'Steven! Steven!' I emerged from my slumber to hear my Mum shouting for me.

'What's up Mum?...'

'You've a letter here, I think it's your marching orders.'

'Sure Mum very funny'. I knew what she meant; in the letter was a rail warrant and air movement papers taking me from a dull Great Yarmouth to a new life with British Army of the Rhine in Germany. The date was 20th November 1973 and I was at home for three weeks pre-posting leave following my two years as a boy soldier, a Junior Leader Royal Engineer based at Dover and also a brief spell in 56 Driver Training Squadron in Farnborough and Crookham Hampshire where I'd taken my heavy goods class three driving license. So far the three weeks hadn't proved to be that successful.

Only a week before I had driven my MG Midget sports car through the wall of the Bradford-on-Avon district hospital while on the way back from a party in Monkton Farleigh, Wiltshire.

Bruised and battered I had slowly coaxed the remains of my pretty little car back to Norfolk knowing full well that Mum and Dad would be furious and wouldn't help one iota toward the rebuilding costs.

Only three months before the crash I had borrowed what seemed at the time a colossal sum of £350.00 to buy the car from a local garage. The car was on the forecourt for £250.00 the other hundred pounds was used to buy the insurance. I had borrowed the money over a three year term at £15.00 a month plus a colossal interest rate. God when I think about it now, it seemed a fortune.

On 'L' plates I had taken the car with my mate Les Dixon back to our training barracks in Farnborough Hampshire. Where, following the two years at Dover as a boy soldier I was finishing my last 6 weeks of Combat Engineer training with the Royal Engineers.

I had only passed my driving test three weeks before on my first attempt in a 3 ton truck; chuffed to rocks at my skill behind the wheel I really considered myself the dogs-bollocks.

My mate Smudge Smith and I had passed on the same day and then found we had been posted to the same barracks in Germany, leaving on the same flight from Luton. Me to 16 Field Squadron, 23 Engineer Regiment, Roberts Barracks, Osnabruck and Smudge to 43 Field Support on the same camp.

Agreeing to meet up with Smudge in Luton for the flight out I said a few sad goodbyes to my remaining old mates from the previous two years and driven from 3 Training Regiment west to Winsley in Wiltshire, home to generations of the Burt family before they upped sticks and moved to find employment for Dad in Norfolk.

A visit to my gran and old school mates, a few parties and hopefully a couple of shags before boarding the 'Squaddies' charter flight with Britannia airways to Gutersloh.

The week in Winsley had gone well until my last night. A Saturday night party in my honour held in the Queens Head pub in Farliegh had ended with everybody piling into their cars to continue the revelry at Ruth Godfrey's house.

Much to my annoyance Glyn Witchard, completely pissed had fallen into the single passenger seat in my car. I liked Glyn, he was an all right guy and one of the crowd but it was the lovely Ruth to whom I had promised a lift and I looked on dejectedly as I saw her walking with my mate Jeff toward Sticky's Hillman Imp. Fuck! Now I'm going to have to work hard to win her back.

So it was just before midnight that we roared away from the pub.

Drink drive laws at that time were very lax; seven pints and you were still ok. I had drunk that and more and God knows how much Glyn had drunk he was completely out of it rolling around in the passenger seat. I knew I would have to drop him off at his house before going on to Ruth's. Hopefully I would get him there before he chucked in the footwell.

It was on a right hand bend before the hospital that I lost control of the car; spinning into the wall and throwing Glyn out of the door and into the road. Seat belts were not compulsory in 1973 and it was a miracle that Glyn ended up completely unscathed. Probably due to the fact he was totally inebriated.

Later while lying in his hospital bed he threw the police into confusion by insisting he was the driver. What possessed him to go off on that tangent I will never know.

Fortunately the first Copper on the scene was Mr Eskdale a special from Winsley who had known me and my family since I was born. When I told him how much I had drunk, he blew into the bag for me and when the full time Coppers from Bradford turned up he gave them the crystals and said I was ok. He then took me back to Grans. I'll be forever in his debt.

After dropping me off I watched him drive away and then hobbled round to Ruth's to let Sticky and Jeff know what had happened. Both said they would come with me in the morning to retrieve the car and see what condition Glyn was in.

With this arranged and Ruth forgotten I limped back to grans relatively sober for a cup of tea.

By nine in the morning we were back at the car that was on the verge where we'd left it. The bonnet was crushed and the entire left hand side floor pan. But the engine was fine and started first time. The left front tyre had been punctured by the buckled wing, this needed bending out and the wheel changing. I was then able to drive the car into the hospital car park. We walked into the ward expecting to find Glyn still in bed but surprisingly we were told by the duty Sister he had been collected by his Dad. The three of us left, Jeff holding my grans transistor radio which had been loose in the door pocket and ended up in the field along with Glyn's left shoe. We had a bit of a laugh about that; I left my car in the car park and in Sticky's Hillman Imp we drove round to Glyn's.

His mum let us in and while giving us a verbal bashing led us into the front room, there we found a very sore and bruised Glyn His mum finally shut up and went off to make a cup of tea. Glyn couldn't remember much. He remembered the shock of waking up

9

in the hospital, not knowing where he was or what had happened. He then whined on about having to hobble out of the hospital with only one shoe and the fact that it was the only pair of good shoes he owned. He brightened up a fraction when we gave him the other one back.

We headed home after our cup of tea and had a slow day checking over my motor for the journey back to Norfolk. I rang my mum and dad whose words 'I've no bloody sympathy for you' I'd expected and retired to the Seven Stars in the village for a quiet beer on the Sunday night.

I climbed into my motor at seven in the morning, twenty four hours behind my planned return to Norfolk. Slowly at no more than 50mph I crawled down the M4, round London on the north circular road and north through Royston, Newmarket and Norwich arriving home in the late afternoon to a subdued welcome.

Fortunately both mum and dad realised that in two weeks I would be off to Germany for an unspecified length of time and that the long term out of favour policy used so often when I was a school boy would only produce a bad feeling round the house. I had left home two years before and had mastered the art of surviving on my own quite well. Even though at seventeen I still fucked up big time I knew that I had to get myself out of it by my own resources.

'I've had a word with Bob'; dad grunted across the dinner table.

Bob Mosley was another chicken farm manager who lived up the road. A man who wore a permanent grin and never seemed daunted by anything; disorganised and scruffy in every part of his life he was a nice bloke and when it came to cars and 'bodged' repairs there was no one better.

'Oh..? What did you say to him?' I replied, trying not to sound too cheery.

'Well I told him what a mess you've made of your car and how you did it.' I kept quiet at this point; I knew dad would carry on without prompting.

'He's coming round tomorrow after feeding to have a look, see what can be done.' (Feeding, as in his 60,000 broiler chickens, not his family).

Brill! Great news, if anyone can sort this mess out he can. These were thoughts going through my head while giving my dad the expected downcast look and mumbling 'thanks dad' into my plate without looking up. 'He's making no promises you know, I've told him what a bloody mess you've made of it, and told him if he had any sense he would leave you to sort it out on your own.'

These were the set piece sentences that I, and hundreds of other kids were used to hearing from their parents and I knew at this point that a sealed lip policy was the best option.

'Well thanks anyway.'

'Eummp,' grunted my dad, 'thank Bob not me.'

These were my dad's final words on the subject for that evening. But as I got down from the table I knew the script had gone exactly as predicted, with Bob on-side something may be salvaged from the wreck of my car and the outstanding £350.00 I still owed on it.

Back in the present I dragged myself out of bed, threw my towelling robe over my shoulders and slouched teenage like into the kitchen.

It was 9.30 in the morning. My Mum had just walked down from the sheds where she was working with Dad to put the coffee on for their mid-morning break. Pete my younger and slightly more sensible brother was at school.

'How are you feeling?' Asked Mum. She could show a bit more compassion now with Dad out of the way.

'Ok... a bit bruised but I'll live' Ahhhh wrong words...

'Yes my lad, you will - Glyn too luckily for you. I hope this has taught you a lesson, you could have easily been killed the pair of you, and if it had been Glyn you would have had to live with it the rest of your life. Remember what happened to your Uncle Ralf?'

'Yeah, ok mum, I hear what you're saying, and yes I have learnt my lesson.'

Drunk one day behind the wheel, my favourite uncle had driven his car through the plate glass window of a hair salon killing a woman under a drier in curlers. He was banned from driving for twenty five years.

'Your letters on the table and here take this tea.'

'Thanks mum.'

Phew, we had moved on to other things.

I sat with my tea and opened the official brown envelope. My mum was correct; it was my movement orders, a warrant for the train journey as far as Kings Cross in London where I would catch the military provided coach transport to Luton. Also included was an air transport movement order authorising my flight on a military charter with Britannia airways to Gutersloh.

The Royal Engineer Field Squadron I was joining was based in Roberts Barracks Osnabruck; 16 Field Squadron. This would be my home for at least the next three years.

The chicken farm on the main road in Ormesby St Michael was not my home. I'd lived there for less than 3 weeks prior to my departure two years before for Old Park Barracks in Kent. Unlike my brother who had joined the local secondary school and made friends in the surrounding villages I knew no one in the whole county. Over the previous two years my 'leaves' or in civilian terminology end of term holidays from Dover, had been spent most of the time in Winsley with my gran. Short periods in Norfolk at home with my brother and parents were ok, but I'd quickly get bored and want to get back to work.

It would have been just the same this time if I hadn't a car to rebuild.

Bob Mosley and I, and eventually, after cooling down, my dad; spent my two weeks at home working on the car.

I bought a complete glass-fibre front end – combined bonnet and wings that hinged from a bracket bolted on the chassis in front of the radiator. I also had to buy a new near-side sill, head light and side light.

Bob promised he would prepare the car and paint-spray it when it was finished. The difficult part was rebuilding the smashed and crumpled near-side foot-well. Bob meticulously carried this out using 3mm thick sheets of galvanised steel cut with tin-snips, bent into shape and pop-riveted in place. This galvanised sheeting was supplied in 6 foot by 1 foot lengths by Buxted; the sheets would be clipped together to keep the baby chicks in the sheds from leaving the area of the gas brooders until they were a couple of weeks old.

It was an incredible piece of DIY sheet metal engineering and he spent a few hours with me on this project every afternoon. When he left to go home he would give me instructions on what to carry on with and how to do it. He was a really dead-on bloke.

There was only one problem... the car would never pass an MOT; the work had not been welded, only pop-riveted; it would fail the safety checks on structural integrity... However the car had been MOT'd before I bought it in June so the annual safety ticket still had seven or eight months left to run. Bobs advice... slap on the underseal good and thick both inside and out and get shot of it.

So after almost fourteen days I signed the car registration document allowing my parents to sell on my behalf; left Bob and my dad finishing off the few little jobs and boarded the train to Liverpool Street in London. It was November 27th 1973; time to be off.

In Transit

It was sleeting that morning as mum took me into the station. The rain and snow mix continued all the way to London Liverpool Street and north bound up the M1 to Luton airport. The countryside from the coach window was slowly turning white as I looked out watching the dull miles slip by.

I dismounted the bus, entered what was then a pokey little terminal and fought my way to the departures board.

The small waiting area which in 1973 was really no bigger than a village hall was packed. As well as charter flights, Luton dealt with many, if not the majority of squaddie flights into the various airports in Germany. We would come to know these as 'Pads flights'. A Pad was a married service person. When referring to anything to do with married personnel whether it was families, buses, flights, houses, whatever, they were 'Pads' and worst of all were 'Pads Brats', (kids) who seemed to be totally without discipline, manners, or regulation of any sort. (I've just alienated 99% of my readers... sorry). At this moment in time it was like some bomb had gone off; kids running round screaming in undisciplined and uncontrolled riotous play. Women, mostly unaccompanied, chattering and shouting to each other while babies bawled in their arms. I'd never seen anything like it, it was more like a refuge processing centre than an airport, but I'd get used to it over the years because regardless of whether the flights were on time or delayed the chaos always seemed to be the same.

I made my way through the throng to the flight departures board and looking up I could see the reason for this chaos, many of the flights showed as delayed; what a bummer.

I looked for my flight due to leave at 1630, but as yet we didn't have a check-in time; but it was still two hours to take-off so we may be lucky.

If all flights were delayed at this time in the afternoon it was quite likely that the later flights would be cancelled altogether.

I was standing there thinking what a pain this was when I had a tap on the shoulder. It was Smudge.

14

'Fucking turn-up this is,' was Smudge's opening shot. 'We won't be flying today you know. Look at the back-log of flights, it's already three-o-clock and there's no let-up in the weather.'

'And it's good to see you to mate' I sarcastically replied. 'Well if we don't fly we'll have to take the coach back to London and stay in the Union Jack. *The Union Jack is a joint services hotel near Waterloo station. Refurbished and extended in the early eighties into double and family room accommodation, in the seventies it still consisted of dormitory rooms in a building that resembled a Victorian warehouse where service personnel in transit could billet for the night.*

'Not bloody likely mate, I'll call my bro, he'll take us back to mine for the night and bring us back up here tomorrow; we just got to sit around till our flight is posted on the board. Then if it's knocked back I'll call him.'

Smudge lived in Welwyn Garden City only a short hop from the airport.

'Sounds like a plan mate, let's find a corner to sit down.'

Smudge and I sat smoking and talking to each other, he was nervous; he'd never flown and never been out of the UK. I'd never flown but I was a seasoned traveller and could talk in passable German. (I'd better explain that my mum is German, I have heaps of family in Germany and had travelled extensively in Europe during my childhood and adolescence). What we were going through didn't really bother me. I reassured Smudge.

'Listen mate, it's not a problem. We board the plane at this end, land in Gutersloh, board a bus and get out in Roberts. Believe me there's fuck-all hassle involved in it...' little did I know.

I finished my cigarette; 'Stick with the gear Smudge I'm going to change some money and I'll go and ask what the likelihood is of us getting out of here today.'

It was the era of the strong Pound; the civilian exchange rate was 4.5 to the Deutsche Mark – I say civilian rate because those stationed in BAOR were paid in Deutsche Marks directly into a German bank account and the BAOR service exchange rate was one

Deutsche Mark more at 5.5 this preferable exchange rate plus the living overseas allowance was a hell of a boost to our monthly salary. I changed twenty pounds and then fought my way through to the RCT (Royal Corps of Transport) movement desk which was overwhelmed with Pads wives bombarding a very harassed Sergeant with questions; I elbowed my way to the front.

'Gutersloh flight Sergeant, any news?'

'You'll be flying later son, they'll be calling you to check in on number two any moment now. Its lack of snow clearing and de-icing equipment, things don't ever change, I see this every bloody year. It's November – its winter what do they expect? Cloudless skies and thirty degrees? Whether or not you'll land on the other side is another matter it's chucking it down over there as well, with real snow, still that's someone else's problem.'

This was his parting shot as he turned his attention to a woman with a screaming brat on her arm. I quickly backed away.

I made my way back to where Smudge was waiting with our gear.

'Let's get over to check-in two mate. They'll be opening any minute.'

Eventually we checked-in, went through passport control and entered departure.

Neither of us had flown before so I was quite excited as we boarded and found our seats. Seat belts checked, safety briefing given, we sat back chatting and waited for our food – our first meal on an aeroplane. It was an evening flight so we got a hot meal with a cellophane packet containing a knife, fork and spoon. As I opened it one of the plastic utensils must have had a sharp edge and I managed to slice open my finger; only a small cut but the blood went everywhere. I wrapped a napkin round my finger while Smudge rang the overhead bell for a hostie. *Well I couldn't reach could I, I was mortally wounded.* First aid administered by the trolley-dolly and a new blood free tray in front of me I tucked in.

While we were eating the captain came on the address system to inform us the flight would not be landing at Gutersloh;

the weather was atrocious and they couldn't keep the runways clear. Pretty good for a military airfield eh? Good job the Ruskie's don't know of the British inability to fly in snowy weather. They may attack in winter...

We would be landing at Hannover; RCT movements would be dealing with onward travel.

After a split second of shocked silence the chatter level had increased tenfold, obviously the military personnel and families came from a wide area; Gutersloh serviced many garrison towns Bielefeld, Munster, Minden and Osnabruck to name just a few. Buses would normally be laid on to all these towns from the airbase. Also many people drove to Gutersloh and left their cars in a parking area. Families were discussing the turn of events across the aisles. This was 1973 long before mobile phones, notebooks and Ipads; you couldn't just text hubbie and say *'hi love plane's been diverted we'll be landing at so and so, could you jump in the motor and collect us.'* No, in lots of ways it was a far more sensible era, but slightly more complicated on the communication front.

'Shit' said Smudge. 'What will we do?'

'Don't worry mate, they'll have to get these people home, they'll either lay on buses to the different towns or a couple of buses back to Gutersloh, let's just wait and see.

It wasn't long before the Captain was back on the address system. There would be an RCT movement's desk in Hannover airport arrivals. Buses would be laid on to take personnel back to Gutersloh or other final destinations.

We landed, entered the terminal – a proper terminal not like the cricket pavilion that was Luton - collected our cases and kitbags from the carousel and searched for further instructions.

Give them their due, the RCT movements people did have their act together; the buses were there to take people back to Gutersloh, Celle, Hamelin and another for Paderborn ... However not one to Osnabruck? This was slightly odd as Osnabruck was the biggest garrison town in West Germany.

'Typical,' grumbled Smudge. 'Every-bloody-where except where we're going.'

'Hang on mate,' I told him. 'Don't get so worked up, let's go over to the desk and find out what's happening.'

It was now fast approaching 7pm (we'd gone forward an hour in time from UK time), I was glad we'd eaten on the plane.

'You need to change money Smudge, this could be a long night and you'll need to get some grub later, go change some dosh and I'll see what's happening with transport. Meet back here.' And with that I made my way into the scrum.

Oddly we were the only two singlies (single soldiers) heading to Osnabruck. There were others going to the town - married and single but they had cars left in the parking area in Gutersloh.

I eventually got to talk to one of the RCT guys.

'You and Smith will take the train Burt. I'll write out two movement orders one for the bus from the airport to the Banhof (rail station), another for your journey to Osnabruck, hand them to the conductor on the bus and ticket counter at the station and they'll exchange them for a valid ticket, ok?'

'Yeah, fine Sarg... and when we get off at Osnabruck?'

'Right, when you get off at the other end phone the guard room at Roberts, the duty transport will come down and pick you up. Give me a mo and I'll dig you out the number.'

I stood and waited patiently while he went through a book that must have contained every military phone number in BAOR and beyond. He wrote down the number then started to fill out a travel warrant.

'Where's yur mate? Get him will you I need your numbers for these warrants.' (He was referring to our personal military service number).

I looked round and saw Smudge; I was jammed in with my case and kit bag, I didn't want to move and lose my place, I'd never get back in, so I shouted and waved until I'd attracted his attention.

'Get over here Smudge, we need your number!'

Eventually armed with two warrants and both of us with local money in our pockets, we went outside for the bus to the Banhof -

two young soldiers trying to get home... well our new home and neither of us was anywhere near our eighteenth birthday.

It was still snowing, but it wasn't windy, the weather was heavy with snow, a thick blanket like feathers falling from a pillow, reducing visibility to less than a hundred yards.

The buses were lined up with the illuminated destinations shining from behind the Perspex above the driver; sure enough there was one showing Banhof. We shook off the snow and presented our warrant to the driver.

'Wehrpass?' Stated the driver looking at me.

Now I could speak German pretty well, but this was lost on me.

'Was ist das?' I queried.

'Militärische pass, militärische pass. He said again pointing at his badge on his chest.

Ah, ID card. He needed to compare the service number written on the warrant with our ID cards. Well fair enough I suppose... after all we could have mugged some other squaddie for the warrants.

All sorted we took a seat and after a brief wait we were off through the snow, a half hour journey on a good day, about eight miles but this evening might be a tad longer. Gritters and ploughs had been out and the streets were fairly snow free, not only snow free but traffic free as well. We arrived at the station just before eight with a train due through at eight ten; an hour and a half on the train great, we'll be in Roberts for ten. Yeah right – wishful thinking that was.

As with most things in Germany the train was exactly on time and we got off in Osnabruck at exactly the time stated 21.39 it was still snowing.

Finding a phone box in the station foyer we telephoned the Roberts Barracks guard room to be told the duty driver was on a shout and there were other pick-ups drop-offs for him to do before he got to us, he was running late, hadn't we noticed the bloody weather. Wait in the station bar and get yourselves something to eat; the cookhouse is long closed. The driver will pick you up from there.

Most German large town railway stations are very similar in layout and have within the building a 'Banhof bier stube, a small snug bar serving snacks and alcohol. This was the warm smoky atmosphere that Smudge and I collapsed into.

We chucked our bags in the corner took off our coats and took a seat at the bar. We were tired, dead on our feet and hungry.

'Well mate, let's get ourselves something I'm starving?' I said to Smudge.

'I can't read the bloody menu can I,' he moaned at me.' I knew that was coming...

'Hang on a mo and I'll translate it for you.'

The barman came over.

'Was Trinken Sie?' He asked.

'Beer Smudge?' I asked my friend. Smudge had his head stuck in the menu and just nodded. Smudge was well out of his comfort zone and not happy; a beer would get him back on track.

'Ja, zwei bitte,' I told the barman.

'Helles oder Pils?' He was full of questions this guy; however the common drink in northern Germany is Pils. A lively lager type beer that's served in a tall thin .3 of a litre glass with a large head.

Osnabruck Banhof in the late sixties.
The 'Stube' is to the right of the main doors where you see the umbrella's.

It's poured slowly bit by bit and you can't be in a rush if you want one. Behind the bar there is usually a row of half a dozen taps with glasses stood under each being continually topped up. Helles (light beer) however comes in .25, half litre or litre sizes and is poured much the same as any other lager, only with a deeper head.

'Zwie habe helles,' I told the barman; two half's of lager; I was thirsty and didn't fancy sitting looking at the beer being poured like John Mills and his crew at the end of the movie 'Ice cold in Alex'.

I'll quit the constant translations now as I guess you got the picture; I can talk and understand German...

I talked Smudge through the menu and ordered us some simple food, bratwrust and pomfritt's.

There was a lovely atmosphere in the stube, people were coming and going, chatter and laughter were all around us, the smell of food, beer and cigarettes; I was happy to sit here for ever.

The barman had asked me a few questions and I'd told him we were new in town and waiting for our transport. He asked me how I came to speak his language and I told him of my German roots. Two fresh beers appeared compliments of the house. I was already beginning to feel light headed.

A waitress came through with our food and we retired to a table to eat.

It was almost midnight before the duty driver got to us and when he did we were both well on the way to being drunk.

We both clambered into the back of the long wheelbase Land Rover and headed through town. The roads were white, at least a foot deep in snow, snow swirled in the headlights reducing visibility to mere yards with no let-up; nothing moved on the streets; the driver crept along in four wheel drive asking us questions; where we were from what was the weather like over the other side. He then told us we'd be spending the night in a cell.

'What!' We both exclaimed as one.

'Yep, we won't be taking you over to your squadrons tonight, it's too late and to shitty, one of the guard will march you over in the morning.'

It was gone one before we eventually got into a bed, in a cell, in the guard room at Roberts. We'd been given a brew, we had the standard two pillows, sheets and blankets, our bags were in the corner and fortunately the corporal in charge hadn't commented on our inebriated state. At least the cell door was open.

There were around ten cells the walls solid with the doors made of bars. Similar to the guard room at Dover these were short term cells for squaddies receiving up to 28 days for minor offences. Longer term confinement for serious offences meant incarceration at Colchester Military Prison. 'The Glass house'

As I lay there in the semi darkness (the lights in the cell area were off but in the front office area they were still on) I reflected back over the last 2 years of my young life.

Military life had started at just over fifteen years old on September 16th 1971 I was on the train to London, then on to Dover in Kent to start a career as a Junior Soldier with the Royal Engineers.

Three weeks previously our family had migrated from our farmhouse home in the lovely county of Wiltshire to Norfolk, where my parents had taken joint jobs as broiler farm managers with 'Buxted Poultry.'

This move was due to major job stability concerns at my father's place of work, 'Marcos Sports Cars' in Westbury. Failing at school and unsure of any post-school direction, I had returned home from a careers day and announced to my parents I was going to be a Junior Soldier in the army; not only a Junior Soldier but a Paratrooper!

They never sat me down to a lecture about how stupid I was, neither was I dissuaded from my plans. Once they had returned from the ceiling and after the 'not over my dead body, we'll tell you what you will and won't do,' parental type lectures, negotiation took place resulting in my parents' acceptance of my decision.

Although the Parachute Regiment was discarded along with wildly optimistic ideas that my parents had of me joining the Medical Corps, the Army Pay Corps, or the Intelligence Corps; all well above my IQ grade, we settled on the Royal Engineers. A Corps of Gentlemen who would utilize my mechanical aptitude and raw but obvious leadership skills... At least that's what the recruiting Sergeant said.

The pre-selection had taken place; first minor interviews and tests at the Army information office in Bath, then a far more rigorous weekend selection at the Signals Regiment based in Corsham just up the road from where we lived outside Trowbridge.

What had prompted me to make this momentous decision? Well I had always been a free spirit, but that childish free spirit had spilled over into bad behaviour, arguments with my parents and brushes with the law, to the point where it was disrupting family life and giving my parents major concerns.

I hated school, my grades were terrible and I had no idea what to do if I left school. I would have enjoyed working at Marcos with my dad, but that was out of the question, the work situation at Marcos was very unstable, our reason at this point in 1971 for leaving Wiltshire and moving to Norfolk.

Then on that school careers day I'd spoken to the lad in the Junior Parachute Regiment and the flash light had gone off in my head; that's the life for me!

Mum and dad saw my departure to the army as a way for me to channel my energies, to get some discipline instilled in me and at the same time get a foundation in a worthwhile future civilian trade. Oh! And of course I would be someone else's responsibility not theirs... harsh but true.

So, following my two years as a boy soldier I'd 'Passed Out to three training Regiment Farnborough to finish a final six weeks of Combat Engineering and a driver training course and here I am a very well trained Sapper holding a B2 combat Engineering qualification, a radio op B3 and HGV class 3 driving licence.

Coming in the Roberts Barracks main gate. 23 Eng Regt cookhouse, with 43 Fld Sup Sqn behind. The education wing is opposite side of the road to the cookhouse, 23 Regt buildings are through the barrier around to the right.

Roberts Barracks - Original Name - Winkelhausen Kaserne from the name of Colonel Winkelhausen who was the German Commandant during World War One: It was then renamed after Field Marshal Frederick Sleigh Roberts.

In 1973, when I arrived it was home to two Engineer Regiments - 25 & 23 as well as support troops - Royal Electrical Mechanical Engineers (REME), Field Ambulance, 43 Engineer Field Support and an Engineer Tank Squadron, 31.

Welcome to the Squadron. Day 1

'WAKEY FUCKIN WAKEYYY!' Shouted the duty corporal grinning through the bars. It's Wednesday 28th November; our first morning greeting in our new Regiment.

Like it or not we were part of that mornings guardroom routine. We'd had four hours kip at the most and things were buzzing.

The members of the guard not on duty, like Smudge and I, were shaking themselves awake, as were the couple of resident internee's. It was 05.30 - breakfast began at 0600.

Smudge and I would be taken over to the cook house for breakfast along with the prisoners.

We clambered out of our pits, threw on our civi's and folded our bedding on the mattress.

The prisoners were taken outside at attention one behind the other and to our relief we weren't told to form up with them. The lad in charge pointed out the cook house door and told us to make our way over. The snow had been cleared from the area in front of the guard room and from the road but on the pavements it was almost knee deep and it was still coming down.

'Eat and get back here pronto we were told.'

As yet nothing was moving and it was still dark, lights were coming on in the barrack blocks and we could just make out the layout of the buildings.

Sticking to the snow covered cobbled road, we made our way to the cook house. The two offenders passed us in double quick time holding mug and nosh-rods in their right hand. I realized we had no nosh-rods, mine were in the bottom of my kit-bag.

'I hope we can borrow some rods,' I said to Smudge. 'I don't fancy going back to dig them out the bottom of my bag.'

'Bound to,' was Smudges quick reply.

Through the main gate a straight road led directly between the two regiments to a 'T' junction at the far end of the barracks where I was later to find the many rows of garages that housed our section APCs (FV432 armoured personnel carriers) and Ferret scout cars; toy's we'd yet to be introduced to. To the left of this road 25

Regiment surrounded a large parade square to the right 23 Regiment was almost a mirror image. (*APCs are pronounced APPS as in apps on a mobile phone*).

Two doors led into the cookhouse, a door facing us in the end of the building and a main door leading off the road. The snow on the pathway leading to the end door had not been cleared so we followed the guard escort in through the front, up half a dozen steps and through a set of double swing doors; we were now in the canteen with the hot plate over to the left.

Just as we had in Dover we queued with a tray. When we reached the first Chef behind the hotplate we told him of our lack of irons.

'He ungraciously went to look for a couple of sets asking us our Squadrons before handing them over and telling us to make sure we brought them back.

'Obviously very valuable rods.' Whispered Smudge...

'I fuckin heard that wise-ass,' came from the Chef. I told Smudge to shut up or we'd be eating with our fingers.

Plates full with a massive fry-up we sat with the guard to eat. The questions came thick and fast and in return Smudge and I asked our fair share. Both 43, Smudges Squadron and 16 were pointed out through the window; just visible through the snow and half-light of dawn. The guard were from 31 Armoured housed above the BFPO, the British Forces Post Office, across the road. Although their block was on the 25 side of the road they chose to eat in 23s canteen. The food was better. *Three years into the future I'd find this to be true when 23 and 25 amalgamated to form 2 Armoured Division Engineer Regiment. 16 would then be rehoused in 31s block and eat in what was 25s cookhouse. 31 moved to Munsterlager and amalgamated with 26 Armoured Engineer Squadron forming 26 Corps Armd Engr Sqn.*

The canteen was filling up and it was getting light outside. Smudge and I made our way back to the guardroom.

'Bring your bags down here lads, I'll phone your Squadrons and get someone to collect you.' The duty Corporal informed us.

We waited roughly ten minutes before a Lance Corporal came through the door to collect... as it turned out, me.

He introduced himself as Lance Corporal Clarke 'Nobby'. I told him my name; wished Smudge good luck and grabbed my bags.

'Here you better let me help you with one of those,' said Nobby taking my issue case off me.

'It'll be lethal out there, till we get the pavements cleared.'

'Is it normally like this in November?' I asked him as we staggered along the road toward 16 Squadron block.

'We get a fair amount of snow through the winter, but we haven't had a dump like this in November in the two years I've been here. We normally end up with snow during FTX but that's because our training area is in quite high country around Kassel.' He replied.

'What's FTX?' I asked.

'Our major annual exercise; but I'll explain it to you later - this block we're passing is RHQ, also houses the Sergeants mess the Regimental tailor, barber and QM stores. We'll take your gear straight to the room; you're in one troop, in my room; it's pretty empty at the moment just three of us, the other guy Ginge Moran, he's a Sapper, he's married and he'll be moving out any day now. Paul Rickard, he's another relatively new lad has already fixed himself a local girl and is living out.

I'm guessing you're an ex Junior?'

'Yeah Dover,' was my one word reply.'

We'd arrived at the double door entrance to the second block. Lads were still bundling out carrying irons and mugs, it was still early - 0720 and breakfast was in full swing.

'Hi Stevie,' someone shouted. 'Welcome to Sixteen.' I looked up to see Geordie Goldsmith from my JL Course 8; great to see a friendly face and I shouted a quick hello.

It was good to be back in the dry. Following Nobby we climbed three flights to the top floor turned left through another set of swing doors and walked the length of the corridor. As I followed Nobby I was receiving cat-calls and whistles. 'Wayhey, who's the new boy then Nobby!? Came a shout through an open door and 'Christ not another ex-Fred,' someone else shouted.

'Take no notice,' advised Nobby, 'ex-juniors always get stick for the first week or so; you'll be ok.'

My new room was the last on the right before the toilets.

There were five beds in the room plus a table and some chairs. The lockers were far nicer than those we'd had at Dover, wooden not metal with a large top box.

'Ok, you've eaten, I haven't. I'm going for some grub, stay here, and get washed and changed, showers and sinks are half way along on the left, Ginge should be back in a few minutes. We'll skip parade; I'll be with you today, show you round and sort out the stuff you need to do.'

With that he was gone.

Only a few minutes passed and a lad came in and sat on the bed in the corner behind the door.

'Hi, I'm Paul - Paul Rickard, you must be Steve? We've been expecting you.'

I shook hands with him.

'Everyone calls me Banjo,' he said. I thought it a strange nickname but never asked why.

'Is that your pit?' (bed space) I asked.

'Yeah, but I don't live in. I've a girlfriend in town and I shack up with her. I moved out almost as soon as I got here, I hated living in the block, its noisy as hell, and the general pastime's getting pissed every night. You'll be sound asleep, then at one in the morning all hell breaks loose when a pissed-up party return from wherever; there's a prize asshole as well who made my life a bloody misery when I got here.'

'How long you been here?' I asked.

'Four months - it's not a bad troop, most of the guys are dead-on, just watch out for MacM, he's a prize fuckin twat and will pick on the new lads. You'll need to stand up to him from the word go or he'll make your life a misery, he did me.'

'Thanks for the heads up.' I said.

'You've not got much of a bed-space there mate, rather than cart another mattress and bedding set up here, get Nobby to sign mine over to you, I was handing my stuff in before the end of the week anyway, take this corner, it's far better than being stuck in the middle of the room. You'll just need to change the sheets and pillow cases.'

'Thanks, I'll do that,' I replied.

At that moment a couple of other guys wandered in, they were Pads who'd just got off the bus and hung out in the singlies rooms until it was 0815 and time for parade. All were wearing combat jackets which were damp from the snow. I was introduced to Alfie Doyle and Flash Hall. Then Ray McKeown stuck his head round the corner, ex-B Squadron and another of my Course 8 comrades.

'Stevie, how ye deein? So you're in 1 Troop eh?' Ye missed FTX ye jammy git. Still NBC practice tomorrow mate ye diny miss that did ye?' He was another Jock from Lossiemouth in Scotland. They were all asking me questions and chatting among themselves, other guys were peering in the doorway to take a look at the new arrival. Ginge Moran and Nobby both returned from scoff and then suddenly at 0815 all but Nobby left to parade.

I was now in uniform with my nosh-rods and mug retrieved from my kit bag and laying on the bed.

'Fancy a brew?' Asked Nobby.

'Yes please, I wouldn't mind one,' I replied.

On the table was a kettle, Nobby went to fill it up.

'You'll find adult service much different to the Juniors Steve, I'll explain all the workings to you during the day as I show you round. We got three troops… one and HQ troop are on this floor; two and three are below. Below that are the office area, armoury and big briefing room. In the attic we have storage this end and a Squadron bar the other, it's open every evening and we hold Squadron functions up there as well. The armoury and briefing, or training room, whatever you want to call it is this end of the block – offices the other end and in the cellar are the troop G10 stores, bedding and signals.'

'Hell that must be some cellar,' I said.

'Yeah it's the complete length of the building and goes back under the road both front and back; the other end – RHQ end, has a vehicle ramp down the side, the trucks and small stuff can reverse down which makes loading easier, it's heated down there as well, I'll take you down later, introduce you and show you round. Each troop has a couple of toilets at the end of the corridors and in the middle as you've already seen are the two washrooms with showers and baths. We rarely have room inspections; rooms take it in turns to clean the ablutions and bogs and we don't necessarily do them every day. However they are expected to be kept presentable by the rooms tasked to clean them. Our SSM Bill Dunn will walk round the lines during the day, if they're not up to scratch that's when we've a room inspection and if he's really pissed off with what he finds we may find ourselves doing it two or three days on the trot. We're woken between 0630 and 0700 depending on where the duty screw starts and how many blokes he yaks with on the round; breakfast is 0630 to 0800, parade out front at 0820; married personnel otherwise known as Pads - who at the moment are in the majority in one troop, get brought in by bus. They're a pain in the ass because as soon as they get in they come up to the lines and hang out in our rooms. They tend to forget this is our bedroom; they'd have a fucking fit if we went round theirs at seven thirty in the morning and sprawled out in their kitchen or bedroom. Still they're a decent bunch who will, at times, turn up with a packet of biscuits to replace the tea and coffee they cadge... you finished your drink? Right grab you jacket and let's make a start. I'll take you down and introduce you to Bill Dunn, he's ok. I'll take you to the troop office, you'll know our troop Staff Sergeant he's just come from B Squadron at Dover, Fred Ludlow... du know him? About eight foot fuckin tall.'

I was in 'A' but I do know him, he taught Combat Engineering and drill for 'B' Squadron.' I replied.

'That's right; our Troopy - well he's a one pip wonder who knows fuck-all, most of them learn on the job from the troop NCOs his name is Timmy Wray, not been with us long either; a bit of a

Jack-the-lad with his Lotus Cortina but again a good enough bloke. Engineer Field Squadrons are pretty informal Steve. Guys are expected to be switched-on, know their stuff, if so things go along very smoothly. We've only got one fly in the ointment in this troop and he's a lance-jack called Paddy MacM a prize dick and pain in the ass; love's giving the new lads a hard time.'

'I've heard,' I said. Banjo told me before you came back from scoff.'

'Well don't let him get to you. Walk away from him if he gives you grief, he'll only do it when no one else is around; typical bully.

16 Sqn block looking from the NAAFI

He really got to Banjo, he's only been here a few months but he's found a German lass in town and moved out already, lucky sod, not may German tarts get tangled up with squaddies so don't hold yur breath on that one. Banjo though – he's a bit of a 'Mod' got all the flash clothes and the prefect fuckin hair-do; that's probably why MacM picked on him... Talking of Paddy's, you know we've a Sapper tour to Londonderry next June?'

'No... I didn't know that... what's a Sapper tour? I queried.

'Four month active service tour in an Engineer role... basically we're in Northern Ireland in a support role to the Infantry. We were there two years ago in Belfast in an Infantry role. It was a shitty four months I can tell you. This one, rumour has it, should be better, we're being billeted outside Derry on the old Ballykelly airfield. They have a proper NAAFI and hold discos. We didn't get that in seventy two when we went as infantry. Ok let's go.'

We left the room and descended to the offices. The first stop was the Troop office, Nobby knocked at the door and saluted.

'Morning Sir, morning Staff; Sapper Burt, came in this morning, I'm showing him round.'

I had a chat with my Troop officer and Staff Sergeant; Fred Ludlow had left Dover as our Course 8 had passed-out in August. He told me there were plenty of ex-JLs in Sixteen; many from 'B' Squadron. The two of them made me feel welcome, said I would be a driver with the Troop for the near future, we'd see how things panned out, sections would start to be organized after Christmas in preparation for the coming Northern Ireland tour, as a radio operator I'd probably be a section Land Rover driver.

Nobby then knocked at the SSMs door, WO2 Bill Dunn shared his office with the orderly Corporal Roger Farrow; Bill said a few words of welcome before we moved on to the Chief Clerks office. Ron Moody the Chief was a great guy, easy going and friendly, I'd get to know him well twelve months up the road when I'd become OCs driver and hang out in his office for hours daily chatting up the delectable Margret M, our Squadron secretary. His side-kick was Cpl Kev Stokes who I would find out later would sit in the corner of the NAAFI bar every night reading a newspaper three days out of date and supping on a single pint. I can't recall ever hearing him order a second.

Ron told Nobby to get me down the bank first thing and open an account it was the end of the month and with luck my salary could be paid in Germany rather than my UK account. He would go through the paper pushing formalities with me later.

'Do you smoke Steve?' Asked Ron.

'Yes I do'. I replied.

'Come back later and pick up your fag coupon allocation from Kev, Nobby'll explain them to you; we'll see you later on'.

'Right let's get out there,' said Nobby.

There were three different banks within half a mile of the main gate, Sparkasse, Commerz and the Dresdner. I ended up banking in The Dresdner because Nobby banked

Hairdresser to the more fashionable Sapper.

with them. It was and still is a small friendly bank three hundred yards down Bramstrasse on the left side. Opposite, Nobby pointed out a laundrette and Herr Schumacher's hair salon where many lads chose to go for a trim rather than leave it up to the camp butcher. Dare I say the discerning Sapper's Coiffeur of choice.

(I visited Herr Schumacher's shop in August 2007 while on a long weekend in Osnabruck he wasn't there but one of the lassie's working in the salon told me he was still around).

On the way to the bank he explained how the cigarette coupons worked; how to get fags from the NAAFI. We had a 500 cigarette a month coupon allocation, may have even been more than that; we'd draw our coupons from the Chiefs office, go to the NAAFI hand over coupons to the value of the cigarettes we wanted (only in king size packs and multiples of twenty) if the Russkies didn't kill us the fags and booze would. They were tax free and cost around ten pence for a pack! Unbelievable! Even in 1973 this was beyond cheap, they may as well have given them away. In fact all the goods sold in the NAAFI turned out to be tax free; fags, booze, music centres, cameras or cars; all were at very affordable prices. The barrack NAAFI was large but I would discover later the married personnel 'Pads NAAFI' was far bigger and carried a far greater range of goods and food stuffs. *(Guys who didn't smoke would still draw coupons, buy fags and sell them on to German civi's (I was one). However if you got caught doing this you were seriously in the shit. I only ever used half my allocation and would send 400 a month to my uncle in Mulheim, he would pay me a D-mark more than I paid for them so I made a mark on twenty and he saved roughly two mark on twenty... win, win.*

Roberts NAAFI with 43 Fld Sup Sqn behind. 2007

Arriving at the bank with my ID card I opened an account - easy as falling off a log; within a few minutes we left; me with the account number and sort code to hand over to Ron Moody.

To Nobby's surprise I'd conducted a large percentage of my account opening procedure in German; as we stumbled back through the snow I explained my knowledge of the language and my German roots. Along the way Nobby pointed out the Winkelhaus pub on the corner of Quirllsweg and An-der-Netter-Heide the road that ran along the front of the Barracks.

'That's a Sapper hangout,' he told me. 'Further down is Pop's Brocky, it's a schnellimbiss, a schnelly, does bratwurst, currywurst and stuff, great grub, he stays open till around three in the morning to catch the lads coming back from town.' I knew all about Imbiss I'd been eating in them since I was a kid.

'Ok, what we'll do is quickly give these bank details to the Chief then hit the NAAFI, its tea break time.
After break we'll do the camp tour, go and pick up kit from the QM, dump it in our room and then go down the G10 for your sleeping bag. Your best belt, is it 37 blanco'd?'

I told him it was.

'We don't wear them here, they've been replaced with a dark green nylon belt which is naff in the extreme but at least its bullshit free. We'll grab your other one and exchange it.'

Sounded good to me - anything but blanco.

We marched, smartly side by side in through the main gate and down to the block; I gave the bank details to Ron and we went back to the guardroom and the main thoroughfare. On the left side of the road opposite the cookhouse Nobby pointed out the education block.

'You'll be told to attend an induction over there in the next week or so Steve; they're held weekly for all first timers to BAOR. They basically warn you about loose women, catching the clap and giving military secrets to girls you're in bed with; although heaps of lads don't bother going... that's going to the induction – not to bed with girls I mean.'

I couldn't believe what I was hearing.

'What do you mean? I asked.

The 'Commie's' plant girls in garrison towns to collect information from innocent squaddies; 'sleepers' they call em. They'll have their own flat, share one, or have a controller to pass the info back to, like a surrogate mum and dad. I don't know if this shit is Kosher or military intelligence paranoia – a contradiction in terms anyway, but the general consensus among the lads is if they can get a shag by telling some bit of totty their short of warm socks or their morale is low then bring it on.'

'Short of socks?'

'Mate, we're fuckin short of everything. Every time we go on exercise we have to tow vehicles out the barracks. Make-do and mend mate and that includes socks 'Fred Karno's fuckin army' that's what we are. Ah well, you'll find out soon enough... moneys not bad though – what with the exchange rate and the living overseas allowance.'

During this conversation he'd pointed out the WRVS, the British Forces Post Office on the lower floor of 31 Armoured

Squadron and the block housing my two mates Smudge and Taddy; 43 Field Support; one either side of the 'T' junction.

His passing comment was,' they're lucky fuckers, you have the life of Riley in a support Squadron.'

We'd arrived at the entrance to the NAAFI and similar to Sixteens block we went up a short flight of steps and through the swing doors into a large canteen, in front of us were rows of tables. Vending machines stood against the nearside wall and over to the left a roller-shutter hatch enclosed the area where two lassies were dishing out tea's, rolls and buns.

The chatter volume was high and there was a warm friendly atmosphere about the place. Nobby shouted to a couple of lads at a table to keep two seats while we went to stand in the queue.

'Hot drinks from the bar Steve, if you want a can then it's from the machine, you'll need a one buck coin.' *(our slang for the Deutsche Mark).*

'Tea's fine, I need something hot.' I replied.

After being served we made our way over to the table, by now a few other guys were there. I was introduced. Suddenly as a Lance Jack sat down a chill came over the table.

'New boy eh?' Nurther fucking ex-Fred – tosser.' And that was it.

I looked around astounded at the weaselly looking guy with the Irish accent who's eyes were far too close together and guessed this must be the universally disliked Paddy MacM *(this by the way is a change of name, but its close; those around at the time will know exactly who I mean).*

Nobby shot me a warning look – as if to say don't take the bait. But before he could say anything a lad across the table, a lad with a London accent and ginger hair piped up.

'Leave it out Paddy, he's just got here, he's in our troop, let's make the lad welcome.'

'Ah feck-off Vickery,' came the reply. 'Fecking wee boy looks like he's only just out of short pants. You'd better look after him.'

36

'I will. Don't you worry,' replied the lad giving me a grin over the table. *Later Nobby told me the lad was Ginge Vickery – he would become my mentor and friend.*

Tea break over, I was walking down the steps when this hand grasped the back of my neck. It fuckin hurt and I viciously twisted to shake off the hold.

It was MacM again. 'Initiation for you tonight sunshine in the Squadron bar; Nobby'll tell you. You'll enjoy that what with our troop having gas training tomorrow.'

I didn't know what to do. I was no greenhorn and no whimp. I'd always stood up for myself and thought nothing of using my fists when I needed to but this was my first day, almost my first hour; did I really need to prove myself this early on in my new Squadron? It was disheartening. These thoughts I disclosed to Nobby as the two of us turned right and the rest of the troop turned left.

'Don't worry about it right now Steve, he'll be a shit for a while and then he'll move on. As for the Squadron initiation... yeah well that is the case and in most cases it's taken light-heartedly. It tends to get a bit out of hand with MacM. Do you drink beer?'

Yeah course I do, I'm not technically old enough to drink though, I'm not eighteen yet.'

Yeah well that doesn't seem to worry anyone here. What they'll do is line up six bottles of Carlsburg on the bar. You need to drink all six in half an hour. They're .3 litre bottles so it's less than four pints in total. The thing is its lager, it's gassy and it's out the bottle. You'll have a bucket beside you and you'll probably chuck the lot up. Don't worry, all the new guys in all the troops do it but Mc Fungus likes to make it worse by getting the lad to drink what he's chucked-up back out of the bucket. There'll be a few of us there to make sure that doesn't happen. You'll be ok. Pace yourself and when you've finished go down to bed. We've gas training in the morning and that's bad enough without a hangover. MacM is being moved after Christmas anyway so you only need to keep clear of him for a month and then he's someone else's problem.'

I was a bit lost for words and slightly trepidatious of that coming evening.

Still a month to put up with the twat; little did I know - a great deal would happen in that month.

We walked back to the cross roads opposite the WRVS Nobby pointing out the area of 25 Regiment across the road. Turning right we walked down toward a further junction 150 yards away. On the left behind 31 Armoured I was shown the stables. At the bottom of the road we came to another 'T' junction; to the left on both sides of the road I was informed were the APC garages and offices belonging to 25 Regt. At the very end, a good four hundred yards were the REME (Royal Electrical Mechanical Engineer) workshops, the refuelling pumps, the block housing REME singles and the back gate leading onto Romeresherstrasser. In front of us was the 30 yard pistol range.

Looking left and right I could see loads of guys clearing snow from the front of the garages, it seemed this was occupying all spare personnel today.

Here we turned to the right – we were now walking with 23 Regt APC garages to our right. On the left was a large parking area with huge concrete ramps.

The whole area was covered in thick snow and as I watched I saw a Land Rover being driven toward a tree, then suddenly the brakes were applied and before hitting the tree the Land Rover started going backwards. A group of guys stood there cheering. The driver got out strutting around as if he'd won some competition; someone else got in and the same thing was repeated. Nobby and I stood there watching. The Land Rover had a good run up, at least a hundred yards. This time the Land Rover didn't get so close to the tree and the group of lads were booing and shouting wanker! Tosser! and chicken! at the bloke in the driving seat.

'What the hell's going on there?. I asked Nobby.

'Best not to ask', said Nobby. 'That's the post exercise wash-down area and a parking area for the APCs in the summer. Those are lads from 37 Sqn but our lads do the same thing every time it snows... The object is to drive as fast as you can toward the tree, in four wheel drive of course; then hit the brakes, ram the stick into reverse; with the wheels locked and still going forward the tree's

16 & 37 Sqn garages.
16s go from the far end to where the windows are in the roof.

coming to meet you. Then let the clutch out; the Land Rover's going forward the wheels are trying to grip in the snow and take the thing backwards; the idea is to get as close to the tree as possible without hitting it, or breaking the bloody drive shafts in the axles. Bloody morons, the lot for them; if Staff Scott sees them he'll go ballistic.'

'I guess they never hit the tree then?' I asked.

'I don't know Steve, I don't get involved, best not to ask...'

As we walked down the front of the garages a couple of guys shouted hello, Taff Graham who'd been in my intake at Dover, Steph Leach and again Ray McKeown who'd stuck his head through the door earlier that morning. A shout came from behind me and a very familiar face a roommate from Dover Courses seven and eight appeared; Bri Bridson.

'Hello mate, glad you could make it,' he said. Bri it turned out was also in 23 but in HQ Squadron. 'I'll catch you later for a beer,' he said returning the way he'd come.

After the hand-shakes and the 'good-to-see-you's' we carried on our way down the front of the garages toward a row of a dozen snow covered Bedford RLs lined up on what would be the end of the hard standing 'What're those buildings over the back behind the fence.' I asked Nobby.

'Stores mate, all four of them fuckin great stores full of everything we need. This is the biggest garrison in Germany and these buildings, the railway that runs each side of them and the canal, which you can't see from here, service every barracks in the town of which I might add there are a good half dozen, more if you count the couple outside the town. All the stuff comes in here; and unbelievably the whole place is run by German civi's; Mojo's we call em. Fuck knows what they'd do in the event of an attack by the Commies, I can't see them sticking their neck out loading tanks onto flat beds while the shit rains down around them.'

Yeah that struck me as odd as well.

'Right, here's our MT office and store, let's give Scotty and Paddy Brennan a quick hello because this is where you'll be working out of; although one troop's your troop, Scotty'll be your daily boss down here in the MT.'

Scotty turned out to be Staff Sergeant Scott and Paddy Brennan a nice quiet lad from Northern Ireland who'd end up in 1975 being killed in a para gliding accident in Jersey; he was the MT storeman.

I shook hands with both of them. We'll see you on Monday Steve.' Staff Scott said. 'You'll start your driving induction with Taff Baines.'

I was amazed at the familiarity of the NCO's; apart from my brief fifteen minutes in the Squadron offices everyone had called me by my Christian name. It would turn out that for quite a few months to come I would be the youngest Sapper in the Squadron, only by a whisker as Taff Graham who was in two troop had his birthday a few hours before me on the forth of April, he too was born in 1956. I would end up being called Stevie and this abbreviation of my Christian name would stick with me for many years into the future.

Paddy showed me the store and all the stuff that would be drawn and signed for when going on exercise. Without doubt I'd entered a new world.

We walked back to 16 via the front of 37 Squadron block, then around the back of the gym; the swimming pool, the officer's mess, the church, medical and dental rooms below HQ Squadron accommodation.

'Don't for fuck sake walk on the Square, if RSM Horton see's you you'll really cop one.' Nobby briefed me.

Once again we were back at our accommodation. It had stopped snowing and a weak sun was forcing through the clouds.

'Ok, next thing, the stores, let's go up and have a quick brew in the room, get your stuff out of your bags while we're drinking it, then we'll hit the QM; you've no gas mask I take it?' I shook my head.

'Mate, you arrived two days to early, we've NBC training tomorrow so it'll be really in at the deep end – never done that in Dover did you?'

'No,' I admitted.

'Ah well it's the same for everyone, not very pleasant; we get dressed in our Noddy suit and mask and then half a dozen of us at a time enter the chamber. We stay in there for around five minutes, running on the spot and jumping up and down. If your mask leaks you'll bloody well know it. If you're ok after five minutes you stand in front of the instructor take your mask off and recite name rank and number before walking out. It's fucking horrible but necessary; on FTX we could spend hours in our Noddy suit and mask. It's tear gas that's used, it activates on all the damp areas of the body and the fluid in your eyes, hence the name, but if it gets on your skin – sweaty arm-pits or balls, it'll drive you nuts.'

This conversation was taking place while drinking tea and I was cross-loading case and kitbag into locker. Brew finished and best belt in hand we once again left the block, this time for the QMs.

I swapped my best belt - the webbing belt I'd used during my two years at Dover for this odd strip of plastic – basically something cut off a reel. The buckle and sliders were the same as the brass buckles on the web belt but lightweight black alloy. Still there was no work involved with this belt so I wasn't complaining. I signed for a gas mask with two cylinders which came in a small square belt bag. A Noddy suit complete with gloves and rubber over boots.

'You'll find out how to put the Noddy and mask on tomorrow,' said Nobby.

A set of 58 webbing with a second bum roll (to hold the Noddy suit), a poncho and piss-pot, (my Dover issue had been handed in before leaving) a soft peaked DMP (camouflage) cap with ear flaps for wearing on exercise... neat I thought. A hood for my combat jacket and as a member of the MT wing I had two pairs of coveralls (overalls in civi terminology). Loaded with this gear we returned to the block ready for lunch.

I walked over to the Cookhouse with Ginge Moran and Nobby. Ginge was moving out of the block within the next couple of weeks, he was married to Sharon and had a quarter allocated in Belm. With both Banjo and Ginge gone and Eric Brown on detachment with the UN in Cyprus there was only the two of us left in the room. Eric would be returning after Christmas for operation Banner - Northern Ireland deployment.

After we'd eaten I was introduced to the troop room by room; the lads seemed ok but for one, who I've already mentioned, he just lay on his pit without speaking. At 1330 both Nobby and I joined the Squadron on parade all very informal; we broke ranks and I went back upstairs to collect the sheets and pillow cases from Banjo's bed, we then headed down to the G10 where I met Cobby, (Gordon Cobb, Lance-jack 1 Troop) and was issued my sleeping bag. With clean sheets, and with bedding signed for had a guided tour of the cellar. In the Signals store I was introduced to Geoff Pengelly a Sapper and a full screw who's surname was Marsden, I'm sure his Christian name was Gerry or it could have been a nick-name due to – Gerry and The Pacemakers as his surname was also Marsden.

'He's one of you lot,' said Nobby – 'Radio op.'

They both greeted me and told me their boss was Staff Sergeant Vic Cole who was upstairs in the office. Once again they seemed a decent set of lads, pretty laid back and happy enough in weather like today, to be tucked away in the warm cellar store. That was pretty much it. We went back to the ground floor offices where I was shown the armoury, the large briefing/meeting room opposite and the notice board holding part one and two daily orders; I collected my fag coupons and half a dozen air-mail flimsies from Kev Stokes and went back upstairs.

Accommodation lines from the central swing doors. First door on the right is washrooms. Rifle racks in the wall, not used. Toilets at the end of the corridor.

I was left to my own devises the rest of the day I went to the NAAFI shop, upstairs above the canteen and bought a packet of two hundred cigarettes. We paid for NAAFI goods in German D-marks; two hundred fags came to around eight mark - two pound in Stirling. Mind bogglingly cheap; went back to my room and after making sure all my gear was put away started a letter home.

The day's work finished at 16.30 with lads returning to the block and the Pads getting the different buses back to the married quarters. Once again I joined my two roommates for scoff and the conversation revolved around how to drink six bottles of Carlsberg in the allocated half hour. I found this pretty daunting but nevertheless couldn't get out of it. After returning to the block I had a desperately needed shower, I was beginning to smell my own arm pits, I got changed into my civis and continued writing letters home.

Around 7pm I was rounded up by a large group of 1 troop led by MacM and escorted to the Squadron bar, one landing above. The bar was large, stretching half the block length, as you came in the door to the left there were tables and on the right was a built in area holding the crates of bottles and barrels. At the end of this short stud walling (*erected by Billy Bryne*) the bar top swept round to the right with the bar stools; then came more tables and the dance floor.

The whole club was painted with cartoon figures and murals of women in bikini's coming out of the sea... well at least wading out of water. Also there was the odd happy faced dolphin here and there. All the women were stood in the water so you couldn't see any feet... apparently the lack of feet was due to the fact the painter, *(quite possibly M Buksy or Billy Edwards)* who done the paintings couldn't paint them

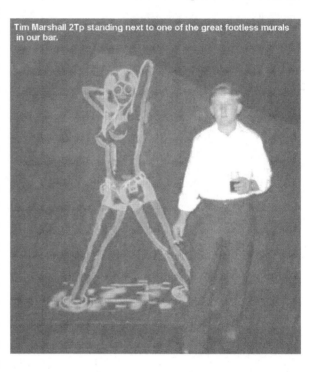

Tim Marshall 2Tp standing next to one of the great footless murals in our bar.

– feet I mean. There was also a juke box. MacM went straight to the box and put on a record; 'Tell Laura I love her' a 60s hit by Ricky Valance. I was to find out this was a record he'd play over and over again, especially when he was pissed to the point it drove everyone crazy. He'd go mental if anyone tried to take it off or told him to quit playing it.

I was given a beer, not that I wanted one, I had six bloody bottles to get through. I was told it was a warm up. Over the next hour the club filled up. Many of the guys were ex-Freds and in the company of ex-Juniors I was not feeling so isolated. Eventually I had my six beers in front of me and forced my way through them. I drunk them within the time limit and managed not to chuck up which annoyed MacM immensely. I awaited my opportunity and made my way off to bed. Hours later I was sound asleep when MacM having left the club and gone to town returned as drunk as a skunk came in and tipped me out of my pit. He thought it hilarious. I thought what the heck it's my first night. Fuck him. I righted my bed, Nobby had also been woken. 'He'll get tired of it soon Steve don't worry. The only other avenue open to you is to front up to him. If you think you can, then fine but I'd wait till you get your feet under the table before you start fighting with a lance jack. He could drop you right in the shit and he's the type of asshole who wouldn't take a beating without getting his own back in some way or other.'

What I didn't know that night of Wednesday 28th November was that within a very short space of time lance corporal MacM would be getting his comeuppance big time.

Pre Christmas 1973

It was a sorry bunch of 1 Troop singles that paraded on the morning of Thursday 29th November.

Following my initiation in the bar the night before, a bunch of them had hit the Winkel and remained there until the early hours; they were suffering. Not that I wasn't - but my hangover was minor in comparison to those around me. It was a grey morning with fine snow falling – more like vapour than anything solid, it was freezing.

We – 1 Troop were on parade in Combats with our belt kit, gas mask and Noddy suit. A couple of trucks were on the way to take us to Imphal barracks for gas training.

We were dismissed; the other Troops dispersed to carry out whatever duties they had to do and we, as a Troop, stood back against the wall of the block while we waited our transport.

Standing there surrounded by the full complement of 1 Troop I didn't feel an outsider or like the new boy at all. The guys were friendly and those lads I'd not met the previous day, mostly Pads, had a friendly greeting. I suppose knowing Ray McKeown helped in this integration. Listening to the conversation it seemed quite a few of the lads hadn't done the gas chamber before, it wasn't just me. Everyone was apprehensive.

Ten minutes and the trucks turned in by RHQ and parked outside our block. Timmy Wray and Fred Ludlow came out and climbed in a waiting Land Rover, our bosses it seemed were not excluded. We were off.

On arrival at Imphal and Mercer barracks we formed up in three ranks by an instructor from the Dragoon Guards. (Could have been the Inniskilling's they were on the point of changing over).

'Good morning men. Cold enough for you?' Came from our instructor.

He received mumbled replies in return...

I thought so – right, its brass monkey's this morning, let's crack-on with this training as quickly as possible and go home. All agreed?'

'Yes Sarg.' We replied.

'So, hands-up, who's never worn a Nuclear, Biological and Chemical warfare suit or carried out gas training?' Our instructor enquired.

I was surprised to see at least half the Troop holding their hand up.

'Ok, we'll go through gas procedure from start to finish as rapidly as you guys can take it in; we'll dress in the NBC suit, otherwise known as the Noddy suit and when I'm satisfied we'll take a break. Trust you're all ok with that? No comments? Good:

In the event of an attack by Eastern Bloc forces it is considered highly likely this would be preceded by, or coupled with, a gas attack. Being able to rapidly and correctly don and wear your gas kit is imperative to your early survival and ultimately the defence of the free west; this gentleman is no exaggeration. (*God the responsibility I had at seventeen years old; defender of the free west no less!*) Initially in the event of a gas attack your first concern is getting the mask over your head and sealed to your face. You will either sense the gas yourself and initiate the alarm, or hear the alarm sounded by someone else; a warning issued either by three blasts on a whistle - the noise of a football type rattle, *he held one up and spun it above his head* or the shouted warning of Gas! Gas! Gas! You do not hang around waiting to sniff the air gentlemen. You get into the mask pronto whether your mucker's bothering or not. The gas you are being trained with today is lachrymator agent or lachrymator, known as tear-gas, sometimes colloquially known as mace, it's a chemical weapon that causes severe eye, respiratory, and skin irritation. It's an irritant used for crowd control and thoroughly unpleasant. The stuff the Ruskies will throw at you will without doubt kill you or cripple you for life or whatever life is ahead of you following an attack. Do I make myself CLEAR!'

Nods and muffled yeses conveyed our reply.

'Good. It is highly unlikely there will be time to dig out either a rattle or a whistle, unless you're already in the suit; it will be a verbal shouted warning so take up the call while getting out your mask and make it loud. In the field the other item apart from your weapon, that you take with you wherever you're going and whatever you are doing is your gas mask; the mask should be constantly attached to your person. The suit is a secondary concern,' our instructor Sergeant continued. 'You may be ordered to don the suit hours before having to use the mask. You may need to remain in the suit for long periods of time, working, eating, sleeping and going for a crap. Get used to it. This gentlemen is serious stuff please do not take this warning or training lightly, it is a matter of life or death. *Fucking hell they never mentioned this in the recruitment office in Bath.* We will now go through the process of dressing in what is jokingly referred to as the Noddy suit.'

We then removed the suit from the 58 webbing bum-role - a pair of trousers with securing straps that go over the shoulder, a cagoule type top with hood. Rubber over boots, white cotton under-gloves with rubber over-gloves and a plastic whistle. The instructor talked us through the dressing and undressing procedure four or five times till he was satisfied.

Noddy suit.

Even on a cold day with the temperature at zero we were sweating; the suits are a 'felt' type material surrounding charcoal and very warm when secured to your torso correctly. They really would be a killer in the summer.

'Well done lads, we'll break for a brew and return here at 1030, the NAAFI is back through the gate, down the road a few blocks on the right, officers are not excluded,' he said looking at Timmy Wray. His parting shot was - 'be careful how much you scoff, you may see it all again in an hour.'

Fred Ludlow formed us up and matched us to the NAAFI where on entry we were cat-called and whistled by the Dragoons... that's army unit rivalry for you, we had to grin and shrug it off.

God it was good to be in the warm.

Tea and buns consumed we were back with our instructor.

'Ok, dress once more in your NBC suits, when you've done this take out your respirator and put it on, do not put the filter on the mask, make sure no hair is trapped between the seal and your face. Good; now place the palm of your hand over the filter attachment point and breathe in. You should feel the mask pulling against your face. If this does not happen gentlemen then take off the mask and readjust the straps; carry on until you form a seal.'

Eventually we all thought we'd got it right.

'This is what will happen next gentlemen – you will put on your mask and while wearing it take one of your two filters and screw it in place; practice doing this while you're waiting. I will enter the chamber and ignite the gas pellets; in numbers of eight you will enter the chamber and walk around; we will do some exercises to get you into a sweat. I will then tell you to take a deep breath and unscrew your filter, put it in the mask bag, take out the same filter, screw it back on, and then forcefully breathe out. If you all do this successfully we'll move on. We will only use the one filter today, once used it will require replacing, there is no need to waste two filters; is that clear enough for everybody?'

'Yes Sarg,' came from us.

'Good; now anyone of you who finds their mask leaking, put up your hand and I'll let you out, you'll return with another group. Do not attempt to blindly rush the door, I will NOT let you out, follow the procedure and I will. *What a sadistic Bastard.* This experience is unpleasant; I suggest you all get it right the first time.'

I was in the first batch of eight; I wanted this over and done with. We all lined up, put on our masks and walked into a very smoky room. All of the other guys with me were standing around the edge of a dome roofed room. You could see the smoke in the air but it wasn't so intense that you couldn't see everyone around you. We did some jumping jacks to get our heart rate up and our breathing faster. Then our instructor sergeant told us to take a breath and carry out the filter change. One lad didn't get it. Either he couldn't align the threads or had taken a breath while the filter was off. He was in  a right old panic and rushed the door. Our instructor wasn't happy and before he was released to the fresh air gave him a right mouthful. The thing is the British army gas mask of the seventies had the filter on the left side. This is because most people being right handed shoot with the butt of the weapon in the right shoulder. If the filter was on the right side it would hinder you when firing. For me being left handed changing the filter was easy however for right handers it was awkward and led to cross-threading problems.

We were then told to take a breath and remove our mask. This was the worse but final part of the exercise.

Everyone held their breath for as long as they could, but your eyes started burning first. I happened to be the unlucky guy who was at the front of the line and everyone started pushing me from behind to get out the door. Some guys started coughing and several were retching. Our instructor, who still had his mask on, yelled at me to "stand still or I'll make you all do this again!" About now, our eyes and noses were running like crazy and we had to take a breath in. This burned like fire and the coughing fits came next. Eyes watering, snot running down our face and coughing like mad, we were finally given the go ahead to walk out the door.

We hit the fresh air, most of us retching and chucking up our beer from last night as well as the tea and buns we'd had an hour ago in the NAAFI.

That was the effect of tear gas, and after a few minutes in the clean air, we were recovering. Imagine if that had been nerve agent or some deadly virus. A few minutes of that and it could very well kill you.

Four groups of us went through the chamber and we all suffered the same indignity of the after effect; but it was a great lesson. Those who flunked it had to go through a second time. There were no half-measures with this training. A serious part of our annual training routine... I wondered how come so many of my new comrades had avoided the chamber in previous years?

We mounted the trucks and departed for Roberts. On the way up to Imphal I had listen to the lads talking about NBC suits, mock gas attacks while on exercise and the time they spent having to wear them. I also got the gist of how exercises worked in BAOR. It seemed that NATO troops of all nationalities had a large field exercise during October and November. These exercises were called FTX – field training exercises. They coincided with the exercises taking place the other side of the Iron Curtain by all the Eastern Bloc forces. We could be in the field anything between three and six weeks keeping a wary eye on what the opposition was up too and ready to take defensive measures should they decide to head west.

Another regular exercise which would take place almost bi-monthly were CPX – command post exercises which were undertaken by only the Head Quarter elements starting in most instances at Squadron or Company level. These exercises would cover many tactical scenario's without actually having troops in the field and would last only for three to five days, war games played out on a map.

We got back to barracks before lunch time, The Pads followed us up to our rooms and slung their gear in the corridor, most had brought in a change of clothes and a towel; our hair and to some extent our clothing still carried the residue of the tear gas pellets. We got showered changed and went for lunch.

In the afternoon, following parade we loosely formed a squad and mooched in step over to the MT section; I went up the stairs along the corridor and reported to Staff Scott in his office. Along with him sat a big built Corporal who was introduced to me as Tom Byrne, Staff Scott's right hand man. In all there were three of them, the third a Corporal Matt Collister, I was yet to meet.

'I'll introduce you to Merv Baines Steve, he'll show you around the MT and explain how things work. You'll sign for a Bedford RL, this will be your truck to run and maintain. Things may change after Christmas but for the time being you drive one troops

G1098 wagon (wagon being our slang for a truck). Taff will explain it all to you. He'll be taking you on your twenty hour transition training and also spend a day with you doing cross country driving on our local training area at Achmer.'

Within a couple of minutes Merv Baines appeared. We shook hands and he grabbed a vehicle works ticket and keys. (*Every military vehicle has a works ticket. The ticket records every journey made, the mileage, the driver, the destination and any fuel that's added to the tank. It needs to be authorised by a senior NCO or a junior NCO that has been given authority. The exception to this is when on exercise; the ticket is then made out for the complete inclusive dates; mileage and fuel used is still recorded for the exercise period.)*

We got to the truck.

'I'm Merv by the way, also known as Taff. You've driven one of these I take it,' he questioned me. 'The reason I'm asking is the majority of guys who get here from 56 have only driven Bedford TKs and they're nothing in comparison to this bitch. This is an RL, it's a bastard. Hard to start especially this time of year - petrol not diesel; uncomfortable as fuck, crash gearbox on one and two, crap visibility, but it's one saving grace... the bloody thing will go anywhere... Well?'

'Well what?'

'Well, have you ever driven one?'

'Twice, I've driven one twice; the morning I passed my test on a TK I was forced to drive the RL lunch truck from Crookham to Southwood and back again and yes in my very narrow experience of the RL, I totally agree, they are a bitch; I'll tell you honestly I was fucking terrified but I think the lads in the back were crapping themselves more than me.'

Taff burst out laughing.

'In fact on the return journey after lunch the back was empty the only guy who was brave enough to come with me was that bloke walking along over there.' I said pointing to a short stocky lad with flaming red hair walking toward us.

'That's Red McCracken OCs driver, yeah he was over doing a crane course recently. Hey! Red over here!' shouted Taff.

Red walked over.

'Hey mate this new bloke knows you, apparently he frightened the life out you driving the dinner truck back to Southwood a few weeks ago?'

Red looked at me. 'Yeah I remember you, just passed your test on a TK and had to drive the dinner wagon, I was in the front with you.'

'That's right but you rode back with me after lunch, you were the only one who did.'

'Because I missed the other two trucks, that's the only reason.' Replied Red laughing. 'Don't worry mate, you'll be on it in no time. Good luck with him Taff.' He said walking off laughing.

'I did pass first time.' I disgruntling said in my defence.

'It's all a piss-take Steve don't worry about it, Ok let's fire her up and drive around the camp a few times, we'll take it easy and tomorrow go up to Achmer and you can throw her around on the training area. We're not teaching you to drive, this is a twenty hour induction to driving in Germany... well... anywhere they drive on the right actually.

The TK I'd trained on in Crookham was the civilian version of the Bedford MK the replacement for the Bedford RL. It was a diesel, small and compact and in the civilian world used as a horse-box, a coal lorry or local delivery truck. It had a large wrap around windscreen big side mirrors a big bench seat that went right across the cab and a synchromesh gear box (no doubling of the clutch required) it had a small gear stick no more than eight inches in length. It was a piece of piss to drive, easier in fact than the tractor we'd had on the farm in North Bradley. I'd nailed it instantly and passed my test first time. The RL on the other hand was a polar opposite. Uncomfortable with very low single canvas covered seats with a huge engine cowl in the middle of the cab. A six cylinder petrol engine and manual hand choke to start. Small square front windows meant you could only see the road ten yards in front of the cab (some of the shorter drivers among us I found out later actually sat on a cushion!) The side mirrors - almost impossible to adjust so you could see anything at all, waved around on single stalks the size of a ladies hand-bag compact mirror; the wipers the size of a pencil cleared a portion of the split screen the size of a fag packet. Gear stick a yard long, sliding mesh on gears one and two (although this wasn't uncommon on a lot of vehicles at the time, many military vehicles still had a complete crash box). There was even a knack to getting in the thing, you had swing into the seat, a technique that's impossible to explain but will be well familiar to those who drove them.

All the vehicles of the day were rugged uncompromising beasts still very much in the WW2 era; a new more sophisticated range of military vehicle was still on the drawing board. That said, the  *bigger, beastie four wheel drive MK would make an appearance with us very early in the New Year replacing half a dozen of our RLs and they soon proved to be an equal to the old RL when it came to off-road work.*

We walked around the truck, Taff pointing out where to check the antifreeze level, the tyres and battery level the air brake cylinder that needed to be drained and left open at night. In the cab we lifted the cowl and he pointed out the oil filler and dip stick. Closing the cowl I sat in the driver's seat ready to go. It felt odd having to change gear with the right hand.

'Ok, every truck on the yard has its own idiosyncrasy's Steve; they all take a different amount of choke they're all temperamental in their own way, you'll get used to it. See that old beast over there,' he said pointing to a truck that looked like it should be in a museum. That's my truck. The Squadron water bowser. It's fuckin ancient, the paper-work for that truck goes back to the Siege of Mafeking,' he said laughing. 'Seriously that truck was built around the late forties, it's on its last legs and it's typical of the type of shit we've got to stop the Commie's with. If you complain of this wagon being temperamental you wanna try starting and driving that thing. The majority of times I end up being towed out of the gate on exercise you wouldn't believe. By the way it's in gear and the hand brake is off.'

I pulled the choke half out, depressed the clutch and turned the key. The starter turned the engine over and Taff said a little more choke; I eased it some more and the engine coughed like someone on sixty fags a day and slowly farting and spluttering came to life.

We sat a couple of minutes warming up the engine and easing in the choke then we were off.

I didn't really get out of second gear, but we drove around the roads of the barracks Taff pointing out important buildings and workshops and telling me about his own life in Sixteen. We kept this up for twenty minutes before returning to the wagon park. I stopped the engine and went to pull up the hand brake.

'No leave the brake-off and in gear, in this weather the pads will freeze to the inside of the drum. Ok let's go and sign for your tool kit.'

We went back up to Paddy Brennan's store, gave him the registration of the truck and he took me to a shelf loaded with items. I signed for the truck along with a tow-rope, Jack, a wheel brace, an airline plus numerous other bits and pieces including a padlock for the side mounted tool box. One key stayed on the hook in the office. Paddy showed me a rack containing a mountain of cam-nets for all the Squadron vehicles. Racks of poles bundled in sixes. These were supports for the nets to break up the outline of the vehicle when harboured-up and tactical. None of this stuff I'd done at Crookham and told Taff as much.

'Don't worry, by the end of next week you'll have practiced it all. We'll take a net up to Achmer and I'll show you how it's done. One thing I forgot, chains... have you fitted snow chains before?'

'Yep, we were shown how to fit them and fitted them at Crookham but I've only ever done it on tarmac and not in the snow.' I replied.

'Ok, we'll take a set with us and you can fit them on the training ground, may as well do it now while the snows on the ground and have a practice driving with them at the same time. It takes some getting used to. Right let's have a brew...'

In the back of the store Paddy had a kettle and we sat talking and drinking tea, it was 1600, we finished at 1630 anyway, Taff didn't think it worth doing anymore today.

'What,' I asked, 'do you guys do all day?'

'Well...' Both Taff and Paddy had to think about this...

They looked at each other and started laughing, neither had a definite answer.

'I run the MT store,' said Paddy. 'I do it every day. I come down here after parade – sometimes before parade. I open up and sign stuff out to the lads.'

'That's if you have it,' chipped in Taff.

'Correct, that's if I have it. If of course I don't have it, I'll go through the process of ordering it and remind myself not to hold my breath while I wait for it.'

'As for the rest of us,' added Taff. 'We parade and we do whatever part two orders tell us to do. We may be driving a Troop to Vorden ranges or somewhere else; if that doesn't happen we come down here, clear up, service vehicles, do some painting, play cards, watch some porn.

'What?' I asked. 'Watch porn? Are you serious?'

Oh yeah, someone will bring in an 8mm projector and we'll set it up in one of the garages, watch a couple of porno's; mind you it's a bit chilly for that this time of year, better to watch it in the Squadron bar in the winter.'

I looked at him sceptically wondering whether he was just having me on as the new boy?

'So you're kept pretty busy then,' I sarcastically said.

'Rushed off our feet in the defence of the Realm, aren't we Pat?'

'Indeed we are Taff, indeed we are.' Pat replied.

They were both grinning at me.

'It's not a bad life Stevie, go with the flow. We work hard when we have to but there are moments when not a great deal happens. We're either getting ready to go on exercise, on exercise, or winding down from exercise; but then there's that little bit in the middle... At that point we practice looking busy and acting busy. At the end of January the Regiment has an FFR inspection; 'fitness for role' the month of January will be hell; we'll be scrubbing, mending, painting and repairing everything for a massive two day inspection. We won't have time to wipe our asses eh Pat.'

'To bloody right Taff.' Replied Pat. 'But then it's back to normality or at least as normal as it can get in a Field Squadron in Germany. Like I said you'll get the hang of it.'

'What's 'fitness for role'?' I asked.

'Random inspection by a bunch of officers and civi's... an audit if you like. Everything's inspected to make sure it works as it should, from a sink plug to a bar-minelayer. It's a prize pain in the ass and it's our turn this year. After New Year as well as tarting-up the block, we'll be painting and spraying all the Squadron vehicles, everything's got to be gleaming; anyway let's wander back to the block its knocking off time.'

As we walked back to the block I had another question for Taff...

'Taff, what's the story with the Parka coats? I've seen quite a few guys wearing them but not everyone. Red was wearing one earlier on, they look a real handy piece of kit?

'Yeah mate, they're the dogs if you can get hold of one. They were brought out and issued during the Korean War. That's where they're left over from. Each troop has a few on the books but their like hens-teeth to get hold of... mainly go to the APC, Ferret drivers and commanders; driving in those open hatches in the winter you fuckin need one. You may get lucky after you got some time-in; gotta find someone who's got one and is leaving, then persuade them to sign it over to you when they hand in their kit. Gold dust.'

The Parka was a thick coat with four massive front pockets and a large tail hanging down the back which would keep your ass warm when sitting down. Also it had a flap that unbuttoned came through the legs and buttoned up the front, keeping the body heat in. A large snorkel hood with a wire for adjusting your viewing slot and straps on the cuffs to tighten the sleeves; I wanted one...

Taff was driving home; he had his own car parked behind the Squadron block, a lovely, what would now be considered a classic, 1970s BMW 1602; He lived, like Banjo, with his German girlfriend Jutta in a private flat in town (in fact it may have been his wife... can't remember exactly). *Taff Baines the second, his brother I ended up working with in 61 Field Support Squadron in Maidstone early in 77. I also wrote for a while to his sister who I met when she visited Taff in 1975 when working as cabin crew for Britannia Airways.*

Taff cleared-off home telling me we'd take the truck out in the morning. I grabbed my rods and went across with a couple of other lads from the Troop for scoff.

That evening I was determined to sit and write home, drop a line to mum and dad and a couple of girlfriends. But it was not to be, by now I'd either bumped into friends from Old Park or the word had been passed on that another JL had join the ranks of Sixteener's.

Taff Graham, who'd been in my intake at Dover and whose birthday coincidently was on the same day as mine was in 2 Troop; along with Geordie Goldsmith. Both were heading up the attic club (from this point on I'll call it the bar) for a beer. I joined them. Just like the previous evening the place was buzzing; it was the evening venue of choice and the starting point for late night excursions into town. In Britain the pubs were still on 10.30 last orders and 11pm kicking out, but in Germany the pubs remain serving for the last man standing. Most of, if not all the Squadrons in both 23 and 25 Regiments had their own bar and the closing times were supposed to reflect those of UK law. One of the duties of the officer of the day was supposed to be the checking of the closure of these bars around 11pm. It rarely happened, what tended to happen was the duty officer would pick a Squadron bar at random. The word would have been passed on before the officer arrived, the door would be locked and those inside would be sitting silently until he'd done his door check and gone away. If by some remote chance he happened to catch the bar open; he'd be given a drink, it was a fair cop – we'd lock up and go to bed or down the Winkel. I remember that happening once or twice.

There were no toilets in the bar; if we had a lock-in a bucket would be put inside the door and anyone wanting a piss went in the bucket. Normal opening hours we'd use either HQ Troop bogs, or 1 Troop bogs. Dance night ladies would use one end of the upper corridor, gents the other.

I sat and talked to Taff and Geordie; other guys joined us, Ray sat down with two other ex-B Squadron lads, Kev Steward and Reg Reid and I began to be filled in on the details of the Squadrons program leading up to Christmas. The following week I was informed 1 Troop had their Christmas meal and piss-up at a pub in town. The following week it was the Squadron Christmas function in the bar with a disco; Pads and Pads wives would also join the party. *I would end up getting myself into trouble at both these functions.*

MacM came in, and had to make another underhanded comment about the table of ex-Juniors... however he wasn't quite so gobby with six of us there. I knew there was trouble afoot with him, it was just a matter of when.

After continued repeats of 'Tell Laura I love her' we all bailed out.

'Fucking hell what is it with him and that record.' I asked Ray on the way down stairs.

'God knows,' said Ray. 'Can't believe it's a lost bloody lover; no bloody women would have him - git.'

Again He was right on that score.

Following parade in the morning I formed up with the small squad marching to the MT, this was general practice in the morning or after lunch break. However you could hardly call it marching it was more like walking in step with mixed conversation going on in the ranks – unless of course the RSM was around. The weather over the last two days hadn't improved it was still bitterly cold with continual snow flurries; however the roads and pavements, both inside and outside the camp had been cleared. Our only source of news about the weather... well about anything really was either the radio via BFBS (British Forces Broadcasting Service), newspapers one day old, flown in and sold in the WRVS or news passed on to us by Pads who had a TV at home. There was a TV in the NAAFI bar but at this point in time it was not the NAAFI bar we frequented (German TV only expect for the single BFBS channel, there was no Satellite or cable telly in 1973).

We had a radio in our room, it belonged to Nobby; a thing the size of a breeze block and almost as heavy, a 'Roberts' covered in brown leatherette. I bought it off him the following year and took it to NI, it lived in the section Land Rover. Anyway getting back on track, the weather was whatever it was when you walked outside and news was the stuff that affected you daily; if it didn't impact on our daily routine we didn't worry about it and rarely even knew about it. The current topics were, the marriage of the Princess Royal to a bloke (army officer of sorts) called Mark Phillips, a right ponce we all thought and we were proved right when he buggered off from a kidnapping in 'The Mall' leaving the spirted Ann to drive off her assailants with a handbag. She divorced him and I don't blame her; a big IRA trial in London and a military coup in Athens. The music at the time was crap as well with Donny 'gleaming teeth' Osmond, the Carpenters who wouldn't know one fuckin end of a fret-saw from another and Gary 'one day I'll be famous as a paedo' Glitter making up the top hits of the month. The only decent record was Bowie's 'Sorrow'.

Now upstairs in the warm MT office Taff said 'We'll leave the truck here, we'll take a Land Rover and I'll show you round the town and all the married quarters. Once you're used to driving on the right we'll take the wagon, maybe Tuesday.'

That was ok by me; as easy as I'd found driving round the barrack roadways the previous afternoon the thought of hitting the roads full of German traffic in that bloody truck without starting on something a bit smaller was daunting. With slight relief, I told Taff that for me it was the preferable option. The Wagons lived outside on the yard as did most of the vehicles during the summer but in the winter the other vehicles wheeled and tracked lived in heated garages. Now when I say heated I don't mean you could work in there coat off with your sleeves rolled up, no, it was more a case of keeping them slightly above freezing by running a couple of four inch pipes along the whole back wall of all the garages and pumping through hot water. All the same it was better than working outside and the lads when not tasked on anything else would be down the MT in the garages fussing around their section APCs.

If the Squadron vehicle compliment was up to full strength, which apparently was a rare event, the numbers would be as follows - each troop had four APCs including the command vehicle - Alpha, Bravo, Charlie and Delta; two Ferret scout cars and an RL for the Troop G10 and cook. So the three troops together had twelve APCs and six Ferrets plus Land Rovers and trailers, on top of which there were the vehicles that made up HQ troop, two more APCs, three or four Land Rovers including the OCs, the AOs, a G10 store and cooks wagon, a couple of six wheel very cool bit of amphibious transport called a Stalwart driven by Corporal Paddy Salmon and Tom Byrne; later to be taken over by Kev Steward and of course we can't forget Taff's vintage water bowser. I believe I'm correct in saying we had room to put two vehicles behind each roller door, one behind the other, the same with the Landy's and Ferrets, roughly there were eight or ten garages per Squadron. *(it was a long time ago, if I'm not exact on the figures I apologise).*

We mounted the stairs to the MT office and picked up a set of keys and a work ticket for a long wheel base Land Rover, Tom

Byrne signed off the sheet and we went down to the garage, done the standard checks and headed out the gate.

Osnabruck was a large garrison – as Nobby had told me, it was the largest in BAOR with most of the barracks having been built for the German military at the turn of the century and located in and around the town.

With me driving and Taff directing we started a pretty standard induction route covering all the barracks and married quarters. We never returned at lunch stopping at an Imbiss for a Bratwurst, our final drive of the afternoon being through the centre of town and round the ring route. By the end of the day I was pretty confident driving on the right, I'd been shown the two garrison cinemas, the two Garrison NAAFI's and the large medical room at Belfast barracks that took less severe medical cases, serious cases being moved on to the BMH (British Military Hospital) down the autobahn in Munster.

We handed in the ticket and knocked off for the day. The coming Monday night Part 2 orders informed me, along with another nine of my troop, I'd be part of the duty guard and fire picket. Parade at 1800 in full combats.

Friday evening again it was a session in the bar, where I was informed the following evening, Saturday, a bunch of lads would escort me into town to visit a couple of pubs and clubs wink wink... I didn't have a clue what the wink, wink was all about, but no doubt it was another new-boy initiation practice that I'd just have to go along with. We ended up in the Winkel and I don't remember getting back to the barracks. This was heavy stuff for a kid not yet eighteen.

Neither Saturday nor Sunday were working days. If we wanted we could spend all day in bed and after a Friday night session sometimes not finishing till five in the morning many did. This first Saturday, although hung over I got up showered and with Ray and a bunch of other lads walked over for a brunch breakfast.

We planned our night out which would begin in the bar, then to the Winkel followed by a couple of Taxi's into the Stadt; we would have a Chinky and hit the local number one buzzing disco, The 'Saskatchewan' or as we called it the Scratch. Why this disco was named after one of the more obscure provinces in Canada heaven only knows but it was. I had never eaten Chinese food or for that matter Indian either so this was going to be a new experience for me; little did I know this wasn't going to be the only new experience of the evening.

MacM wasn't coming, what a relief that was; Titch Graham, Ginge Vickery, Derek Stevenson, Cozy Powell, Ray and a half dozen others had all signed up to this evening out, even the table in the Chinky had been booked. The afternoon was spent finishing letters and doing some washing. We had an Indesit twin tub washing machine in our Troop toilet, donated by one of the Pads who'd invested heavily in a new front loading automatic. This was 1 Troop singlies pride and joy and jealously guarded. It was not shared with other troops. If they

wanted a washing machine best they get one from somewhere or someone; ours was not loaned out. This machine turned out to be indestructible over the weeks and months that followed I realised it rarely stopped, during the day lads would come back to the block to put washing in and it seemed to run all night long which was not surprising with a dozen or more guys living-in and needing to wash their gear.

A quick beer in the bar, then down to the Winkel for a couple more and we were in a fleet of taxi's heading into the centre of town and the Chinese restaurant.

In the back of the cab Benny Bennett threw his arm round my neck and in a alcoholic slur asked.

'Are you a virgin Stevie?'

'No.' I indignantly replied. 'Why the hell do you want to know that?'

'That's good, that's good, just wondering, you're in a man's world now, a real soldier mate; it surprising how many of you juniors get here without ever having got your leg over. We have a duty of care you know. We need to know these things to keep you boy-wonders on the straight and narrow. We're proud and happy you've had shagging experience, well done eh boys?' He said looking at the other four jammed in the taxi.'
The whole fucking taxi was cracked up. I of course had no idea what they were on about.

'So who was the lucky lady then Stevie? Schoolgirl sweetheart or what?'

'No it wasn't actually and that's all I'm telling you; and get ur bloody arm off,' I said, shrugging myself out of his grasp.

More laughter.

Ray had told me; just put up with it. Get the first week out of the way and you'll be in – a member of the troop. It's all harmless fun.

We arrived at the Chinky. This was a completely new eating experience for me, I'd never eaten Chinese food before and with ten or more of us choosing from an extensive menu there was a huge selection to try.

Around the table my new found colleagues and friends (in brackets) were discussing where they should take me next... there was a great deal of winking and smiling going on; innocent me didn't have a clue.

'Well I think we should take him there now,' said Titch.

'Yeah now before he's so drunk he can't get it up.' Someone else piped-up.

Get it up? Get it up? What the hell were they on about?
There was much hilarity...

65

'It's only half an hour to wait and if you don't want to sit and wait get some yourself,' said another voice. (more laughter).

Right - hands up for now, hands down for later,' said Ginge.

The majority were hands up.

'Ok, that's settled then. Let's get the bill.'

It was close to ten-o-clock and everyone by now had had a skin full of booze, I'd only had a half bottle in the Squadron bar and two Pils in the Winkel; with the meal I'd put away a couple of half Helles.

Although I was still below drinking age, I'd drunk alcohol for years; in fact dad had started me on a Sunday lunch Mackason when I was only five! So I was still with it and pacing myself. I knew it was going to be a long night and I wanted to keep myself reasonably with it. I didn't necessarily trust the crowd I was with to get me home safely either.

We came out of the Chinky and turned left down the street toward the railway station. *(This part of the town centre is now a pedestrian area, in the 70s it was still a part of the city centre road system).*

A few hundred meters we turned into a side street past the dark entrance to an underground car park *(which I found out later to be a second entrance to the establishment to which we were heading... let's say a less obvious route to 'Sin')* and within a couple of minutes came to a door, we knocked and a huge bloke stuck his head out.

'Wie viele?' he asked. How many.

'Who's in,' asked Ginge

'I'm going in,' said C.

'Yeah me to,' said F.

'Ok guy's money out let's chip-in for the new boy, three bucks each...'

The light came on! We were standing outside the town whore house centre - the Bordello, Brothel, or as it would be called by squaddies the, knocking-shop.

'What the fucks going on?' I asked.

'Part of joining the club mate, the final part of your initiation, a half hour with the girl of your choice, all paid for by your mates... you're not going to chicken out on us are you?'

I sheepishly looked round. If I backed out I'd never live it down.

'What about VD,' I naively asked. 'Won't I catch something?'

'Slim chance Stevie, they all get checked regularly by a doctor, this is state sponsored sex you know, it's not back street 'Hooking', this is sanctioned by the state - top quality totty, wait till you get in there you won't know which way to turn. The old Krauts have it sussed in the sex department.'

The money had been collected; thirty marks for half an hour.

What the heck...

'Ok,' I said grinning, 'let's go.' Lots of well-done's and slaps on the back.

'Drei, mate,' said Titch. 'And this one,' he said pushing me to the front is erstmals (first timer). The door was held open and I went into a corridor. A desk sat just behind the door with a chair. The carpet and décor were smart.

The money was collected by the pimp or bouncer, whatever you want to call him (I didn't get a first time freebie, or a buy one get one free) and we were walked up some stairs to an open area containing couches with a number of scantily clad girls. *(Please note; I have not disclosed who was with me!)*

Fucking hell I thought, I've died and gone to heaven.

We three sat down on the couch, this wasn't the type of brothel you sometimes see on the tele where guys sit around drinking with women draped over their laps and soft music playing. This was your, *'I'm just nipping round the corner for a half hour to let off some steam dear'*, type of establishment; smart, clean but also functional...

The girls paraded around in front of us and believe me we were spoilt for choice. Don't think for one minute these girls were at the back of the queue when looks and figures were dealt out, very much the opposite. Although all tastes were catered for in the size and shape department,

I made my choice and was taken by the hand upstairs. The last thing I heard before leaving the room was the bouncer tell my girl I was a first timer.

She was talking to me in broken English, putting me at my ease, which I was incredibly thankful for; because here was I being pulled up the stairs by a girl at least six years my senior wearing hardly any clothes; my heart was beating like a drum. We entered what can only be called a cupboard with a bed and dresser. She shut but didn't lock the door, walked me to the bed and placed my trembling hands on her breasts.

'Please remove,' she commanded in broken English *(it was like something out of 'Ello Ello')*, slightly confused I took my hands away.

'No the Brassiere, please remove the brasserie.' Ah now I get it; I felt round the back.

'No at the front please,' she was pointing.

This was to be my first encounter with a front loader...

And at this point - you dear reader, are left outside guessing...

When you're only just seventeen and being taken for a ride by a professional, half an hour is plenty long enough. Also time is money to the young lady concerned so it's to her advantage to get you in and out (literally) as quickly as possible. I was very soon back downstairs on the couch waiting for my two oppo's. One by one they joined me and politely saying goodnight (I was taught manners by my parents) we left to find our mates in the Kolumbus Keller. On the way there I got a good ribbing from the other two and questioned on the experience; questions that – apart from saying I'd enjoyed myself immensely - I was not prepared to answer.

(I must add here, that at the time of writing the prices put forward by certain individuals for a session at the Eros centre varied considerably. My recollection was 30dm for thirty minutes, I know that's what my new mates paid for my induction that night I was taken by the troop, and I'm sure I paid that when forcibly dragged there on other occasions).

The Kolumbus Keller was exactly that - a cellar bar on one of the towns many 'old town' back streets. It was popular with squaddies and locals alike, unlike the Scratch disco there was rarely any trouble; I think squaddies took pity on Helmut the one armed bouncer on the door, they didn't want to give him any trouble with his single arm impediment; saying that he was a bloody big bloke. A one armed bouncer... never ever came across another one... Bouncer that is not spare arm.

Over the coming three years I would spend many hours at this bar and others...

Frank Butler reminded me of Big Maggie a monster of a women who would hang out in The Oxo Bar... *'She was German with a Scots accent, I believe that she once married a Scottish squaddie. She was bald but wore a wig if you could call it that, she was always trying to pick up some poor unfortunate guy. Frightening!'*

Baz has something to add to this... *'Big Maggie; used to drink pints of brandy and orange... She saved me one day when I was flaking out by the door. Some Turk was trying to lift my wallet. Maggie spotted it and I awoke to a massive thump as she'd twatted his head against the wall. Appy days.'*

'Yes Baz they were; but I'd just like to add that other wallet lifting nationalities are available.'

I also got this from Pete Adams, thanks Pete... I *Remember when I was Squadron Duty Cpl (at that time with 31 Armd) went up to close the Sqn bar. As I went in the door I saw her there and thought - Oh shit this could be big trouble. She looked at me and asked, 'Are you here to close the bar?' I said, 'yes.' She replied. 'Well if any of these lot cause any trouble give me a shout and I'll sort them out.' Was I glad she was on a good mood as I'd seen before how she could sort out anyone who upset her. What a character.*

On arrival I was clapped down the stairs by those less frustrated individuals who'd saved thirty marks and bought a beer.

The plan had been to have a few beers here and then go on to the Scratch; however when the question was posed, who was staying, who was going? It turned out to be half and half, some wanting to stay where they were, others wanting to disco.

I really didn't fancy a disco and elected to stay where I was, I was knackered and well on the way to being legless. Around one-o-clock we found a taxi and headed back to Roberts.

This kind-of wraps up my first weekend. Sunday was a slow day with a few of us in the evening walking over to the town military cinema on Barbarastrasse next to the big Pads NAAFI to watch 'American Graffiti' and grabbing one of Pop's lovely bratwursts on the way home.

We'd left for the flix through the back gate over by the refuelling point, but on the way home to get to Pops we had to walk around the perimeter fence where I spotted the German war memorial below. I asked my mates the history of the memorial but none of them knew much about it. Judging by the inscription it would have been built after World War two. The location seems odd as looking back through Roberts Barracks history the camp was occupied by Allied forces as soon as the surrender and occupation of Allied powers took place. I would really like to know more of the history of this memorial...

The following week I carried on my driver induction training.

On Monday I began with another driver as Taff was tied up with something else. My new assessor was a huge Fijian lad (at least I think that was his ancestry) called Anthony Stevens. His nickname was Tojo or Toj (pronounced Toej); another lad married to a German girl they lived in the married quarter area of Kline London. The Monday was spent again in and around town in the Land Rover.

That evening I knocked-off at 1600 and went back to the block to prepare my kit for guard duty. The dress was full combats with beret, less cam-scarf. The less than attractive plastic No2 dress belt was worn around the waist. I can't imagine why we needed to do that; either we had a belt that was functional, our 58 belt for example, or no belt at all; someone on high must have been under a delusion that we looked more presentable this way for guard duties. They were wrong; combat dress and plastic belt did not go together.

At this time weapons were not carried by the guard patrol and wouldn't be until a major security incident a few years up the road and a mile away at Quebec barracks.

At 1800 we paraded in front of the guard room. As far as I can recall there were ten of us, eight Sappers one Lance-jack and a Full-screw; the Sappers in pairs done two stints of two hours during the twelve hour shift' this included patrolling the barrack and manning the barrier; the NCOs took turns on the desk. It was a big barrack to patrol and it took well over half an hour to do a full circuit, walking slowly of course. We were armed with the deadly accurate - up to two meters, pick-axe handles. These state of the art weapons were in great demand in military barracks all over the world and the company producing them must have worked overtime to supply HM Armed Forces. The advantage these manually operated intruder suppressing weapons had over the more sophisticated SLR was, that unlike bullets, the pick-elve (as it was known) could be used time and again at no cost. *(This to the delight of the Conservative party in power at the time, who were stumbling from*

71

one crisis to another with raging inflation, wage claims of forty percent and Communism knocking on the door by way of the trade unions).

So instead of shouting HEY STOP! Don't move or we'll shoot you - (In English of course – so it was advisable for all intruders to learn English before clandestinely entering a British army barracks). We just crept up behind them and split their skull open... Job done.

We paraded in two ranks to be quickly inspected by the duty Sergeant and officer who dismissed us and returned to the warmth of their respective messes. No one in their right mind wanted to be outside in minus seven degrees longer than they need be. That would be the last we'd see of those two.

Guard duty was pretty uneventful, it was dark at 1800. I was paired with Ginge Vickery and we started the first two hour stint, we would knock off at 2000. During our stint Ginge had told me 'I'm going to show you something on our next patrol that you won't believe.' I said you're not going to flash yur 'dick' at me are you?' I was coming to the conclusion that anything possible in the 1 Troop induction process!

'No,' he said laughing, 'it's to bloody cold for that, but I'll show you something equally as scary,' What the fuck was he on about... I had to wait and see.

We knocked-off and had some tea and toast in the corner of the bunk room. Going to sleep was hard on guard duty at least this early in the evening, the lights were still on, lads were making tea and there was a great deal of noise from the front desk. Guys were heading into town or down the Winkel and stopping to talk on their way past. I read a bit and talked until 2200 then the lights were switched off at least in the sleeping area and I managed to drop-off until 0200 when our duty corporal woke us for our second stint. It was serious brass monkey's outside, minus eight! I was in combats with a hood and a pair of our pathetic woollen gloves – I watched jealously as Ginge dragged on his Parka over his combat jacket; lucky bugger.

Before leaving Ginge asked for the key to the back door of the cookhouse and stuck it in his pocket.

'I know what you're up to Ginge,' said Paddy Holmes smiling.

It was cold and dark, very little moon, freezing snow crunched under our boots as we walked across the road to the back door of the cookhouse. I wondered what Ginge was up to...

We stopped in front of the door, Ginge had is finger to his lips. He took my pick-elve and along with his stood it against the wall.

'This only works on a really dark night, tonight's ideal.' he whispered. 'Keep dead quiet, don't say a word or make any noise whatsoever and above all keep walking, don't stop.'

I was intrigued. What the hell was he up to?

Ginge very quietly turned the key in the lock and opened the door slowly; only as much as we needed to squeeze in and we were through into the narrow corridor that led to the steps leading down to the cellar and up to the canteen proper; this was the rear entrance to the cookhouse. It was pitch black in the corridor, Ginge slipped past me in the darkness and I felt him tug my jacket. He began to pull me toward the steps. At this point two strange things hit me; one was a crunching underfoot; a crunching not dissimilar to the frozen snow we'd been walking on minutes before. But we were inside now, in the dry and in the warm it couldn't be ice under our boots. But with each step the crunching was louder and also squidgy under my boot? The other thing that hit me and had my heart racing was - as my eyes became adjusted to the darkness I could see the walls and floors moving, I thought it was some kind of optical illusion, we got to the top of the stairs walking through the open single door into the open seating area and everything seemed to be moving – the tables, the walls, the work surfaces of the hot-plate, everything... My God what on earth was going on? Ginge made his way to the left, toward the main double swing doors I'd used on my first morning; here was a bank of a dozen light switches to operate the lighting in the main room; the crunching still came from underfoot only more prolific. Ginge hit the light switches.

Fucking hell! I'd never seen anything like it and never want to again. Cockroaches! Billions of them some up to 40mm in length – everywhere; you could barely see the floor for the heaving mass.

I'd stood still for barely ten seconds but looking down the fucking things were already crawling on my boots.

'Bloody hell!' I shouted kicking out with my legs.

But as we stood there looking they vanished – like magic in front of our eyes this seething mass of insects, so prolific we could barely see the surfaces on which they were scurrying about, disappeared; into cracks behind the stainless steel worktops, behind skirting boards, down drains in the floor, into the cracks between the tiles – any minute space available they were in it or through it.

Within the space of 30 seconds the only cockroaches remaining were the crushed carcasses of those we'd walk over - some of which were still trying to drag there broken bodies toward sanctuary. Ginge and I walked back the way we'd come finishing of the wounded under our boots as we went.

'Bloody hell mate I wouldn't have believed it if I hadn't seen it with my own eyes, there's millions of them, don't they ever fumigate the place?'

Ginge was walking toward the light switch.

'Yeah frightening aint it? Like something from a fuckin horror movie, we show all the new boys hahaha...'

'Yeah haha fuckin ha mate – nuff to give someone nightmares for life that is.'

'They fumigate every 6 months or so but it does no good, they're hidden up in place's the fumigator team can't get to; I reckon they been fumigated so many times over the years they've become immune to the stuff.'

We were leaving the building while this conversation took place. I never wanted to go back in there at night ever again. *Even now 45 years on I can visualize that brief 'Indiana Jones' moment of insect horror.*

'If we go back in in the morning all those squashed roaches will be gone, eaten by their own kind; awesome things. Don't let it put you off your breckie though.' Ginge was really savouring the moment... 'No one's died from food poisoning. They're all over the barracks, even in the accommodation – you'll wake up for a wazz in the night and see em scurrying across the floor of yur room – don't let it get to you; they look grim but they're harmless.'

'Ok, ok, drop it Ginge, I've seen and heard enough, let's take back the key and stay out in the fresh air, I'd rather freeze than be in there.'

We took the key back to the guardroom, Paddy and a couple of those still awake joined in the hilarity... we continued on.

Guard finished at 0800 when the Regimental MPs took over the barrier.

We paraded and were dismissed by the duty Sergeant; the duty Rupert hadn't made an appearance all night.

Parade was at 0820 and we the guard missed it. We went up to our rooms, Pads with us, got washed, changed into our everyday work clothes and made our way to our respective work places, for most that was the MT area.

Taff Baines was still not back, so once again I had Tojo as my assessor. He told me that today we'd be leaving the barracks in my RL, my short relaxed initiation by Land Rover was over.

I collected the work ticket and keys and with Tojo watching carried out the pre-use checks. While doing this I was curious as the odd addition on the headlight surrounds; these were a metal rim with sprung loaded twist fixings as if a cover or something could be put over the head light. I asked Toj what they were.

'They're infra-red black-out holders Steve. It's like a round black glass in a metal surround. You push the lugs in the cut-out and twist it, the lugs engage in the slots holding the plate tightly to the head light. When you turn the lights on you can see nothing unless you're wearing infra-red goggles. Then the road ahead is almost as clear as normal night driving. So a convoy could move at night in the dark without giving away a position, all the drivers driving by infra-red light. Which of course is great unless the Reds are using infra-red goggles to spot troop movement then you're stuffed. I've never fitted a set and never seen a pair of goggles so I wouldn't dwell on it, just another aid to warfare we do without. Oh and while we're on the subject of convoy driving at night, come and have a look at this.'

He took me round to the back of the wagon and pointed underneath. 'See that white disk with the number. That's a night time convoy plate and light – the light shines on the white plate and you follow the leader; the idea is if you're too close to the wagon in front the plate disappears from view and if you're too far back you can't see the unit lettering. The light switch in the cab operates to the left and right; left is normal side and head lights; to the right its convoy one click and convoy and side lights on the second click… if of course it works. Ok let's mount up and get on the road.'

For the time being this was my truck and I needed to get used to its idiosyncrasies Tojo sat next to me as I depressed the clutch and turned the engine over while playing the choke in and out, finally it fired, coughed, farted and settled into a more reliable 'I'm not going to cut out' rhythm. We made our way to the main gate, turned left and headed for Achmer.

The day was spent with a mix of country driving and town driving, getting used to the narrower country roads that unlike Britain didn't have Cats-eyes running down the middle. Once again we drove through the married quarters and around the different barracks within the Garrison, as Toj told me you need to know where you're going when in a short time you're let loose on your own. When we got back around 1600 we went straight to the fuel point to top up. Vehicles must be left with a full tank at all times Toj informed me.

The rest of the week I went out with Taff - Munster, Bielefeld/Paderborn, and Minden a different garrison town each day. We went up to Vorden ranges and the Dutch NAAFI at Bramsche. Taff told me the Dutch garrison operated a bank of underground missile silos that ran along the rear perimeter of Vorden ranges. On occasion they would be opened and the warheads raised. *A year in the future while shooting on the range I drove to the far side of the site to collect the red flag; as I drove toward the perimeter fence three warheads appeared from the ground a couple of hundred yards in front of me. Until that time I'd been sceptical of the story. But that day I was gob-smacked to witness this rare event, I only wish I'd had my camera.*

On Friday we chucked a cam-net, poles and a set of chains in the back of the wagon and headed for Achmer for a few hours cross country driving and an hour of camming-up tuition. A real fun day taking the wagon off road and being shown just what it could do and also having a go myself with the chains both on and off.

On the way back to Traz Taff informed I needed to wash down the wagon, but as usual the wash down point across from our garages was frozen solid.

He also said that he would tell Scotty, that in his opinion I could be let loose on German roads unsupervised. I was well chuffed.

It was Friday 7th December and tonight was our troop piss-up, it was being held at a large guest house near the football ground in the Schinkel area of the town behind the railway station. This guest house was used to catering for rowdies and large groups, a couple of lads in the Squadron actually trained and played for the local German team and were familiar with the place. The food was supposed to be really good.

We'd all bunged in for the meal, taxis and probably a few beers as well; when the money ran out we'd have to continue to pay from our wallets.

When I went back to Osnabruck in 2005 I drove around the area again it was surprisingly unchanged and as with most things in Germany the guest house was still there and looked pretty much the same as I remembered it; that in itself is typically German.

Roughly thirty of us piled into the place from a fleet of taxi's ordered to pick us up from the Winkel, so we were all half cut before we even got there.

Eventually we were seated and the evening began; I ordered Jagerschnitzel with poms I remember this because I saw the whole meal again through the big white telescope a few hours later along with all the beer I drunk.

The evening was going well, the food had been consumed and we were all sitting around one big long table laughing and joking including our Troop Staffy and Rupert, Fred and Timmy Wray. I had settled in with the troop and had no concerns, MacM was down the other end of the table and I hadn't given him a thought as I walked merrily toward the toilet.

As I stood there hanging out over the urinal I felt a grasp on my collar, I realised it was MacM shaking me backwards and forwards against the trough while asking me how was I enjoying my evening with real men.

'Eh sprog; enjoying yourself with the men are yee, yee wee boy?'

Bastard...

I tried to shake off his hold and in doing so sprayed piss over the side of the pan which deflected back onto his trousers. I was pretty helpless in this position and the next thing I knew he'd smashed my face into the wall, causing a gusher of a nose bleed.

'Fucking teach you piss on my trousers, ya piece of shit yee'.

The next thing I heard was his cry of pain as he was flung back against the wall; pinned there by Ginge Vickery. Ginge had watched MacM follow me into the toilet and had guessed he was looking for trouble. There was no love lost between these two and I found out later Ginge had been waiting for his chance and a reason for sticking it big time to MacM; this was his opportunity.

Ginge had elected himself my mentor for the time it took me to settle in the troop and this unprovoked attack on me was all the reason he needed.

There and then in that toilet he beat the shit out of MacM. Ginge went at him like a bare knuckle fighter of old and all the time he was laying it on he was telling MacM that if he ever so much as spoke to me out of turn again, or any other person in the troop for that matter the beating would be repeated. In the end Ginge was pulled away by others coming into the bog, but the damage was done. MacM was a mess – split lips, bleeding nose black eyes. Ginge was pulled bodily out of the toilet while a couple of lads lifted Paddy to a sink to wash the blood off his face.

He wasn't pissed; he was a bully and was beaten fair and square. I probably could have sorted him out myself if I'd been in the Troop longer but I was still very much the new-boy and had yet to get in the swing of it. From that moment on though I changed, no one would ever fight my battles again and over the coming years, just like at school and at Dover I could do more than hold my own in a scrap.

MacM left, caught a taxi and went – probably to drown his sorrows in the Winkel; the rest of us continued to party till we could barely stand. In the end with the onset of table dancing; the Zulu Warrior and finally the performance that broke the camel's back 'The dance of the flaming ass-holes', the proprietor politely asked if we would leave. He wanted to get us out before things got out of hand and his restaurant burnt to the ground.

The dance of the flaming ass-holes for the uninitiated comes after the Zulu Warrior song which follows a rendition of the Royal Engineer Corps Song. 'Hurrah for the CRE' this song originated among RE units during the South African War. The words part in English and partly in Zulu are sung to the tune of the traditional South African song Daer de die ding. The Zulu words are a complaint that there is too much work for too low wages and little food. (Nothing changes then).

Good Morning Mr Stevens and windy Notchy Knight,
Hurrah for the CRE
We're working very hard down at Upnor Hard.
Hurrah for the CRE
You make fast I make fast make fast the dinghy
Make fast the dinghy make fast the dinghy.
You make fast I make fast make fast the dinghy.
Make fast the dinghy pontoon.
For we're marching on to Laffan's Plain.
To Laffan's Plain. To Laffan's Plain.
Yes we're marching on to Laffan's Plain
Where they don't know mud from clay.
Ah, ah. ah. ah. ah. ah. ah.
Oshta. oshta. oshta. oshta.

Ikona malee. picaninny skoff.
Ma-ninga sabenza. here's another off.
Oolum-da cried Matabele,
Oolum-da. away we go.
Ah, ah, ah, ah, ah. ah. ah. Shush.....................Whow!

At this point the song changes to 'Haul em down you Zulu warrior, Haul em down you Zulu chief;' (instead of hold him down, the proper lyrics).

The drunken Sapper on the table has, while the song has progressed stripped naked... well perhaps he still has on his socks and shoes but all else has been discarded. The performance could end here to raucous applause and cheers or continue on with a rolled up burning, yes burning, newspaper being handed to the dancer who waves it around his naked body and backwards and forwards between his legs. Hence the name 'the dance of the flaming ass-holes.

There is a take on this where the newspaper is stuffed into the dancers ass crack – both are hilarious to watch.

I might add I never had the bottle to do this but there were those in the Troop and Squadron who shall remain nameless who just couldn't wait to get on the table and catch fire to their anal fluff. Nuff said... let's move on.

Taxis were ordered and we waited for their arrival. Meanwhile a bet was made with Timmy Wray that he couldn't run back to the barracks wearing only his socks and shoes... Remember, we were in the first couple of weeks of December and it was fuckin freezing! Now this was our Troop officer; a rather green Rupert, who I guess wanted to impress his men. In our merry state we collected his clothes and with jeers, wolf-whistles and shouts of encouragement waved him on his naked way. Unfortunately his chosen route back to Roberts was along the main route into town, through town and out the other side. I suppose there would have been a less conspicuous route but Timmy never had a map. Haster Weg and a short cut through Dodesheide onto Bramstrase would have been a more sensible and less conspicuous northerly route home, a lot of it through the married quarters. He was picked up by

80

the MPs just outside the town centre and delivered, still naked to the officer's mess. Had the military police (from here on known as 'Monkey's') been a decent bunch they'd have dropped him off and no more said, however in keeping with tradition they played the prize assholes and after dropping him reported him to the duty officer, who duly reported him to the CO who dished out a substantial fine and two weeks as duty officer as a punishment. We did pay the bet though, which relieved him of small portion of the financial hit.

All was quiet in the Squadron over the weekend; there was no kiss and make up between Ginge and Paddy who stayed in his room licking his wounds.

Monday morning parade and we all turned out in front of Fred Ludlow, Timmy was keeping a low profile in the office, worried no doubt of the raucous reception he'd receive if he appeared.

Wait a couple of days for the heat to die down... at this point he'd not been seen by either the CO or our OC and was blissfully unaware of his forthcoming bollocking..

MacM's beating would not slip through the net either, although nothing was said at the time, the scrap had been noted by Fred and word had also got back to Bill Dunn. An in depth enquiry would need to be held. MacM looked a mess and this could hardly be swept under the carpet; also it would come to light that his nasty attitude toward other less experienced colleagues had been noted for some time. It was time for action to be taken.

Why we paraded in the morning was a mystery, it wasn't as though a 'roll' was called; or that we were inspected, we just formed up. Any news that needed to be imparted to us was given out and generally the senior corporal would call us up and dismiss us to our duties. However this morning Fred came out and informed Paddy, Ginge and myself that we would be questioned by him and Timmy Wray.

MacM was called in to the Troop office first while Ginge and I were told to wait at ease in the SSMs office.

'Keep Shtumm Steve, say as little as possible,' Ginge whispered to me. 'We don't grass mate and they won't expect us to.'

I nodded; I wasn't likely to, I knew how the game was played and what was expected of me I'd keep my answers short and say the minimum.

We were all questioned. When my turn came I was squirming, I had no intension of dropping anyone in the shit and I was pretty certain that MacM had learnt his lesson. However that wasn't how the interview panned out. They were well aware of Paddy's previous behaviour, gripes and complaint's had been filtering back to the Troop officer for some time. I was asked how he had interacted with me during my short time in the Troop and I answered honestly but playing it down. I never said how I'd been warned by Banjo and Nobby on my arrival. I believe both were also called into the office and questioned.

Ginge received a bollocking and four nights guard duty when it became 16 Squadrons next turn. He was lucky not to be fined or nicked for GBH, but things like this weren't broadcast – generally what happened within the Squadron or Troop stayed within the Squadron or Troop; unless it was mega serious. In other words it was dealt with in house.

At the start of the New Year Paddy would find himself transferred to one of the other troops; that had been on the cards anyway. Poor buggers he was now their problem; however he'd been warned his behaviour was not acceptable for a NCO. I never really had any more to do with him or took any notice of him until the coming August and that's another story... maybe even another book.

Driver daily duties – the journey's we were tasked with, were posted on Part 2 orders. We checked these in the evening but most of the drivers knew what they were up to the following day before leaving the MT at knocking off time.

Tuesday I found I was to be accompanying Flipflop, *(Dave Marshall)* our resident barman, to the NAAFI store to collect bar stock; beer, soft drinks, crisps etc. The coming Saturday night was Squadron Christmas dance and disco night in the bar, and a shit-load of booze and nibbles were needed.

The NAAFI stores backed onto Roberts; you literally drove out of the back gate and then right again into the massive stores area beside the canal and railway lines. First buildings on the left were the RMP (Royal Military Police) offices and quarters; passing them you swung round to the right where the NAAFI supplies were kept in a relatively new warehouse. Ahead of us was the huge stores area consisting of four massive old German built warehouses, those I'd been shown by Nobby on my first morning, on one side the rail lines and on the other the canal.

The stores blocks with railway sidings in view

A hard standing area was filled with Engineer and other equipment. I could see Bailey Bridging also MGB parts, bar mine layers and other stuff. As I wrote earlier, unbelievably this whole complex was run by German civilians, the Mojo's; surely this place would be on the Ruskies list for a first strike when the shit hit the inevitable fan?

Dave showed me where to reverse the truck and we began loading up. After a half dozen kegs I asked how much we needed.

'Bloody hell Dave is this just for the dance?'

'Squadron 'do' mate, Pads wife's drink as much as the blokes, we daren't run out. This is only the draft beer - we got bottled beer, soft drinks and spirits yet; cumon get stuck in this is the easy bit, wait till we get back... this fuckin lot's got to go upstairs and you'll bet there're be no fucker in sight to give us a hand. We'll be back again next week to get the Christmas and New Year booze.'

Eventually we were loaded and making our way back; as we pulled out the gate – because there were no road markings – without thinking I headed for the left hand side of the road and just missed a passing truck.

'Stop!' Dave shouted. ' You're on the wrong side!'

I stood hard on the brake. 'Christ, I'm sorry Dave, you ok?'

Yeah, I'm ok it's the booze I'm worried about; fuck that was close, wouldn't have been the best start to your army driving career would it? Costing the Squadron a couple of hundred quids worth of beer and profit. You would not ave been a popular Sapper mate.' He said laughing.

God he was right, my first trip out unsupervised; I needed to keep my wits about me until driving on the right hand side became habit.

We got back and parked outside the block, it was tea break so before doing anything else we hit the NAAFI for a brew. There were a few girls who worked the downstairs counter; a little lass with brown curly hair – Sharon; a larger more robust lass who was Scottish – Edna and a small mousey lass with blonde hair whose name I can't remember, I think she was married to Chris the manager who ran the shop and bar upstairs, they lived on the premises. They were all Pads wives; happy and welcoming and took a great deal of banter from the lads. They also worked evening shift and we could go over and get an omelette, fry or a filled roll – note I say filled roll rather than just a roll... a few who will remain nameless got one of those as well.

Some tea breaks you'd find a wife or two waiting in the canteen and they would sit around the tables joining in the laughter. It was dawning on me that the Troops and the Squadron as a whole was a very tight knit group where even the wives' were included.

Dave went off to sit with lads from 2 Troop and I sat with the guys from MT. Today Chris Seamen's wife Marion had come in with their little girl, I was introduced. As the years went by a group of us would enjoy parties at Chris's flat in Belm and also in Dodeside at Johno and Lynn Johnsons and Pebs and Hilary Hilyers Pad as well as others.

Back at the block Dave and I started lugging barrels of Starlight and Double Diamond up the three flights to the bar; to say this was knackering was an understatement. 'I never considered this when I volunteered as barman,' Dave said.

However we were lucky, Bill Dunn returned to the block as we were on keg number two and rounded up guys from the armoury and G10s down in cellar to give us a hand. I made a mental note to get Tom Byrne to allocate a different driver the following week.

Friday cease of works and Part 2 orders had a list of people allocated to help prepare the bar for the Saturday evening dance. Unsurprisingly as a new-boy my name was on it. After lunch on the Saturday a group of us had to report with an NCO to collect table clothes, cutlery for the tables and the buffet food in trays to be laid out and covered with cloths. The disco was run from behind another curved stud wall partition at the far corner of the dance floor a car was painted on the studwork and the windscreen section of the car lifted out to expose the DJ and the turn-tables; very cleverly done. *(Thanks to Billy Byrne for reminding me of this).* This was how I spent my third Saturday in the Squadron.

My third Saturday and the end of my second full week would see me once again in trouble, however this time it was double trouble... two incidences in one night.

I learnt later it was a set-up and a very embarrassing one; the party was in full swing and I was sat at a table with a bunch of Singlies, Pads and wives'. One of the ladies, a very attractive lass, was sat to my right with her husband on the right of her. We were well into the evening and become worse for drink when I was dragged by this, what was rapidly becoming a vision of loveliness, onto the dance floor for a slow number. She was not slow in coming forward and I soon experienced the rotating thigh treatment... The Cobra was very quickly lifting the lid off the basket...

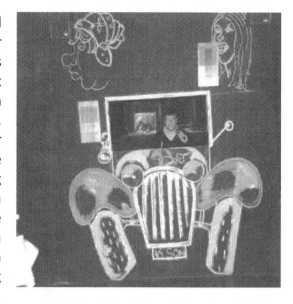

at 17 guys you'll remember that almost anything to do with almost anything female can cause this to happen and I wasn't renowned for my self-control. I was like one of those toy cars that you push a few times over the carpet and the spring gets tighter and tighter... then you let it go; Zooooom - it goes head long across the carpet and into the wall; and I too was just about to go head long into the wall.

Returning to our seats and in receipt of gentle knee pressure below the table-top my response was to glide my hand up the ladies thigh, below, I must add in shame, the ladies skirt. The meandering hand met no resistance, in fact the warm legs parted slightly and I saw it as an invitation for further progress. At this point she turned and smiled the most wonderful smile before informing everyone around the table that Steve had his hand up her skirt. I was stuck completely dumb – couldn't move and realised her legs had slowly closed - trapped... Like a fly in a Venus fly trap I couldn't move if I'd wanted to. Everyone was looking and grinning *(see it was a set-up!)* as she lifted the table cloth to show hubby. (*I know the names of those around the table... I still remember the name of the girl concerned however I'm not going to name names or troop's because? I don't want to be on a hit-list!*).

Her husband, who, I thought would land me the thick end of his arm, just grinned and said 'now, now, Steve that's no way to behave.'

I could have died of embarrassment the whole table was laughing fit to bust and I wouldn't live this down for yonks, if ever. Finally the pressure was off and I got my hand back. 'Would you like a drink,' she said. I nodded – words wouldn't come. I didn't want to lay my hand on the table because it was red and showed the indented marks of her stocking tops. 'I'll give you a hand,' I said... Ahhh! Wrong thing to say! 'You just did,' was her reply; which of course caused further uproar around our table and had those sitting nearby on the other tables looking around questioningly what the joke was about.

We got up to the bar where she ordered a tray of drink for everyone, mine included.

'Sorry Steve, it was a set-up and I led you right into it didn't I, can't blame you really; still you're not slow in coming forward are you...' she said grinning at me. 'Are you going home for Christmas?'

'No I'll be here over Christmas, I'm pretty certain I've no leave left.' I sheepishly replied.

'I'll tell you what, how about having Christmas dinner with us? I'll ask Greg; it'll be nice to have company.' *(I've used the name Greg here because as far as I can remember we didn't have a Greg in the Squadron at that time and I don't want in any way to give any pointers toward those concerned)*. After the somewhat embarrassing faux pas that had just occurred I didn't believe for one minute Greg would want me anywhere near either his flat, or his wife, but I was wrong. On Monday a Christmas invitation was extended.

'Are you sure?' I asked.

'Leave it with me, if you'd like to come, I'll talk to Greg.' We went back to the table.

The buffet was over and the raffle had been called; the music continued. People were moving from table to table I could see Taff Graham my mate from Dover Intake troop sitting at another table with a bottle of spirit in front of him. I made my way over. On the table in front of him was a bottle of Asbach Brandy. Not a .75 litre bottle but a full one litre bottle.

'Jeez mate, are you celebrating something or what?'

Taff was well pissed. 'No, just won it on the raffle and I'm going to drink it all... you'll help me won't you.'

'Sure I will mate...' I was not far of total collapse either...

I woke up with someone alternately slapping my face and rubbing an ice cold bar towel over it. I was on the floor and a crowd of men and women surrounded me.

'Are you ok.' I was asked.

'No I need a bucket quickly,' I slurred. A bucket was brought just in time, with not a millisecond to spare a gallon mix of beer and brandy shot from my mouth into the tub.

'Better out than in mate, let's get you downstairs.'

'Where's Taff,' I managed to get out.

Don't worry about Taff he'll be ok.' I heard as I was carried by a couple of lads toward the door.

For me the party was over.

'Steve wake up, Steve wake up!'

I slowly came back into the land of the living, my head was pounding like a drum and someone had pissed in my mouth... at least that's what it felt and tasted like.

Oh my God, I felt so ill. Nobby was stood by my bed with a 58 mug full of tea, basically a pint.

'Here drink this.'

'What happened, what's the time?' I asked.

'It's gone midday and you mate, decided with Taff Graham to polish off a litre bottle of Asbach. That was following God knows how many beers. You're the lucky one, Taff's in Osnabruck general having had his stomach pumped, we couldn't bring him round last night... wonder he's alive and I'm not kidding when I say that.'

'Oh fuck'. I managed.

'Oh fuck indeed mate. I have a sneaky suspicion that tomorrow you'll be receiving a bollocking second to none coupled with some extended guard duties and a fine... and if you get away with that you're a lucky fucker. You know the OC was there last night? In fact all the bloody officers were there; SSM and SNCOs plus wives. Having a German ambulance turn up at the Squadron Christmas 'do' is not looked on as part of the entertainment. Anyway you've both survived so that's a relief.'

'Do you know Taff's ok then?' I asked.

'The duty driver's gone to collect him was the last I heard. Anyway drink this; brunch is on till 1300 if you're capable of keeping anything down.'

'No, a biscuit will do till tea time, God my stomach is sore... you sure nobody kicked me in the guts?'

'No Mate you puked till we thought your stomach would come out yur mouth, no wonder you're sore. Oh yeah... and what about this wandering hand rumour? Any truth in you having your hand down Sylvi's knickers?' *(name change).*

I groaned and wished I was miles away.

'No, not true... I never got as far as her knickers.'

Hahaha... Nobby was laughing. 'You fell for that one mate; an old 'embarrass the new boy' trick and Sylvi's a bugger for it; ah well you're certainly making a name for yourself if nothing else. You've only been here three weeks and the whole Squadron knows you; brilliant!' He went and lay on his bed chuckling.

I drunk my tea, got up and showered; feeling like death I started to prepare my kit for the next morning. It wasn't long before there was a knock on the door – anyone and everyone was putting their ten penny worth in. I decided to go and see if Taff was back and wandered down to two troop lines. He was in lying on his bed and feeling pretty sorry for himself.

I asked how he felt and told him that if he won the raffle ever again not to get me involved. We discussed our impending bollocking and what our punishment would be. At 1645 I went and got by nosh-rods and walked with a few of my troop mates to the cookhouse.

That evening I stayed in the lines, wrote some letters and done some dhobi.

'Graham, Burt, fall out to my office!' The SSM was on Monday morning's parade and he was not letting any grass grow under Saturday night's antics. We fell-out from our respective troops and walked smartly up the steps and through the swing doors.

'You first Burt. Graham - wait in the Chief's office.' The door was closed behind me.

'Any driving duties detailed today Burt?'

'No Sir.'

'Good – following this discussion you'll report to the bar upstairs and spend the day clearing up. Right Burt, the story from your own lips.'

I told what happened... well as much as I could remember.

'Your name has come to my attention twice in seven days Burt. You were involved - although I'll admit not to blame, for the fracas at one troops Christmas function last week; again where alcohol was involved? You may have noticed in the short time you've been here Burt that alcohol is readily available, dare I say it, it's almost freely available because the stuff costs next to nothing whether you drink it in the barracks or in town. Many young soldiers who are posted to BAOR get dragged into a strong drinking culture and I don't want this happening to you. Both you and Graham have come to the Squadron with excellent reports from your junior service. In fact I've noticed you were both in the same intake the same Squadron and you're both the same age to the day? That itself is significant because both of you are still five months away from your eighteenth birthday – which I'm sure you're aware is the legal drinking age in the UK? This I will be passing on to the OC for his information when charging you at 1330 hours this afternoon. I hope – for your own good you stay out of trouble and if your name should cross my desk again it will be for the right reasons. Do I make myself clear?'

'Yes Sir.' I replied.

'Good; outside this office 1330. Now send Graham in and report to the bar for clean-up duties.

I turned and opened the door to hear his parting shot... 'And I suggest Burt, you keep your hands to yourself.' I cringed, although there was an element of humour in his voice when he said it.

I walked to Ron's office and told Taff the SSM was ready for him. 'Don't worry I whispered,' as I left for the attic.

Flipflop and I waited for Taff before getting stuck into the cleaning. Cutlery, crockery, steel trays had to be returned to the cook house; table cloths to the laundry. Glasses washed, the floor mopped – everything; it would be a day's work for us. The small attic windows had been opened to allow fresh air through a room that stunk of stale beer and cigarette smoke. We talked among ourselves, the majority of conversation revolving around what would happen when we appeared in front of the OC at 1330.

Lunch came and went and we found ourselves outside the SSMs office. He didn't say much, told us to leave our berets on Roger's desk and wait outside the OCs door.

'Right you two plonkers, this is how it works. I'll call you up, left turn and in quick time you'll march into the office, swing to the right and wheel across in front of the OCs desk; I'll command you to halt and right turn. You'll remain at attention looking ahead and only speak when spoken to. When the OC has finished I'll give the order to right turn and in quick time you'll right wheel out and into my office where I'll tell you to halt. I will then say my few words and dismiss you. Understood?'

'Yes Sir.' We answered in union.

Accused! Accused SHUN! (I'd been through this once before at Dover). For Taff this was a first time. We stood ramrod stiff, me behind Taff while Bill knocked at the OCs door, stuck his head round and said a few words. The door was left open. I could look directly across the passageway into the Chiefs office where Ron and Kev Stokes looked on grinning.

'Eye's front Burt!' Bill roared at me.

'Listen in and remember what I told you. Accusedddd in double time quick MARCH! Eft-ite-eft-ite-eft-ite...' We entered the office, swung round in front of the desk.

91

'Accused HALT! RIGHTTT TURN!' The OC sat before us reading notes on his desk; he looked up...

'Burt, Graham; I must say it gives me no pleasure at all to have the two youngest soldiers in the Squadron in front of me on my orders. However, antics such as happened at our Christmas function Saturday evening cannot be ignored and must be nipped in the bud. Burt I find looking through your Dover record *(Known as the Confidential)* that you've previously been on OC's orders for a drink related offence? Perhaps you'd enlighten me to what happened in that instance?'

I then explained how I'd been caught in a pub in Dover while celebrating my (very short lived) promotion to junior lance corporal.

I caught a glimmer of a smile between the OC and the SSM who was stood behind us.

'Graham - drinking antic's such as those you both were involved in, can and have resulted in death. You Graham may have come very close to drinking yourself to death on Saturday night. If that had happened it would have been my sad duty to inform your parents; I would also have had to explain why a Sapper in my charge had drunk himself to death while still under the legal drinking age. Also by involving the German civil authorities you brought both the Squadron and the Regiment into disrepute, I was reminded of this by the CO in the mess... I however feel stronger about the former consequences than the latter. This incident has highlighted the fact that we have Sappers joining us in the Squadron, and of course other Squadrons as well, who are not old enough to drink and to some extent I feel we are responsible for allowing this situation to occur. Under the circumstances this cannot go unpunished; however, it was a prank that went horribly wrong with no maliciousness intended.

Do either of you have anything to say in your defence.'

'No Sir.' We replied together.

I am therefore going to charge you twenty pounds each; you will also be banned from buying alcohol in the Squadron bar until your eighteenth birthdays. When the Squadron is next involved with barrack guard duties you Graham, will carry out three consecutive night duties and you Burt, three consecutive nights as duty driver. I don't wish to see you in front of me again. Especially you Burt.

March them out Sergeant Major.'

'Accused SHUN! Righttttt TURN! In double time Quick MARCH! Eft-eit-eft-eit-eft... and out we went back into the SSMs office where we halted and were stood at ease.

'Right you pair; I'll be talking to our bar staff and putting them in the picture regarding your ban. I'm sure it was an oversight on the part of the OC but he failed to ban you from the NAAFI bar and it hasn't occurred to me either... Get back upstairs and finish off with Marshall. Tell him that he's not to serve you alcohol; it will be published on Part 2 orders. Now get lost and stay out of trouble, especially booze related trouble.'

'Bloody hell moaned Taff as we walked back upstairs. 'Twenty quid – twenty bloody quid, that's a fortune; you won't be getting a fuckin presie from me this Christmas mate.

'Don't moan at me, you're the one who had the brandy,' I retorted.

Yes twenty pounds was a great deal of money, almost twenty percent of my monthly wage; bummer indeed.

We filled Flipflop in on the details and finished off the final cleaning. The bar was ready to reopen.

On the way back from scoff I read Part 2 orders; sure enough there was mine and Taff's name and our OCs 'award' for the want of a better description.

I had also been tasked for the rest of the week to drive a truck load of blokes 50 miles south to Sennelager ranges, a huge training area to the north west of Paderborn. Here a mock town had rapidly been constructed to benefit troops training for Northern Ireland deployment. The whole place at this time was made from single skin corrugated iron; rows of streets with doors leading into nothing. From the front - upper and lower level, window type apertures looked onto streets below. Behind these windows were scaffold walkways where volunteers could rain down bricks, stones, rotten tomatoes or stale bread and all sorts of other crap onto the Squaddies being instructed in check-point procedures, street clearance and crowd control below.

'Tin City' as it was called, was still evolving with the 'Tin' element of the mock town slowly being replaced by full blown houses with rooms, stairs, back yards, roofs and alleyways exactly like the real thing, the terraced streets of Strabane, Londonderry or Belfast.

Crowd control. Tin City

At the time Engineer units from all over BAOR were involved in the construction of this training establishment and prior to Christmas 1973 we had two sections working on and off at Sennelager.

In the coming six months I'd find myself there many times; not helping in the construction but on the ground with riot shield and SLR doing very realistic training for our tour to Ballykelly in the coming June. Even though it was a training establishment it was very realistic and foreboding - with burned out vehicles on the streets and barricades that would be set on fire during the live training. Where they got the volunteer population from to play the part of rioters and petrol bombers I don't know, but they certainly put their heart into it; injuries were not uncommon.

In the morning I collected my wagon and drove round to the cookhouse to pick-up the lunch time Hay-boxes and bread. (I'm sure any ex-service personnel of the time will remember the lovely bread in the pink waxed packaging, with the blue mould flecks running through the middle? Courtesy of the British army bakery in Bielefeld (Royal Army Ordnance Corps).

Tin City was my detail for the rest of the week and I was getting into the swing of things. On the route home I'd pull the wagon over in the village of Halle where a road side Schnell-imbiss sold the most wonderful currywurst, bratwurst and Shashlik. We'd scoff a mountain of this quick food and on arrival at Roberts go in for a full blown evening meal. With all the stuff I consumed including gallons of beer, peanuts and crisps I continued to remain as thin as a rake.

For those who had little or no 'Leave' left for a Christmas break, me included we had the standard two days off and went back to work between the Christmas and New Year. However I had a couple of days still owing and having heard no more of a follow up to the invitation to Greg and Sylvi's, which in a way was a great relief, decided to visit my gran in Mulheim. As Christmas fell on the Tuesday I went to see Ron Moody and asked for the Monday as a leave day, plus a local warrant for the train. We were entitled to three or four local warrants a year free of charge, local meaning to travel within BAOR. Most of the lads never bothered to use them. In fact I doubt they even knew of the availability, I did; because of having family an hour away on the train I'd looked into it early in my arrival. I phoned my gran to tell her I would be coming down on the Saturday, duties permitting.

At the end of the week I caught a taxi to the Banhof and headed south to see my gran, uncles, aunties and cousins.

We paraded again for work on the morning of the 27th; I'd retuned after lunch the day before catching one of the few trains running on Boxing Day. On the Saturday I'd changed trains in

Dusseldorf for the short onward journey to Mulheim but on Boxing Day my uncle had dropped me off at Dusseldorf Station.

There was not a great deal going on these few days between Christmas and New Year, the few dozen of us not on leave would make the most of it; we all knew that on January 2nd we'd have a month of graft ahead of us for the Regimental FFR.

New Year's eve found us in the bar – us, as in every Sapper living-in. Tonight would be a mega piss-up lasting into the early hours. I'd looked at Part 2 orders and the guard, duty SNCO and Rupert were from 25 Regiment next door. It was highly unlikely that they would be aware of Taff and my drinking ban. Still we were both very sceptical and reluctant to get ourselves in the shit again until someone pointed out that our punishment as published, stated we were not allowed to buy alcohol in the Squadron bar. It never said anything about anyone buying it for us or about us drinking it. Therefore as the ever growing and happy crowd pointed out we had fuck all to worry about.

Whatever Corp or Regiment you belong to, if you're a single soldier in your barrack block at Christmas or New Year you're going to party. The singles contingent of 16 Squadron were no different.

Every Squaddie left in the block descended on the bar - or should I say ascended to the bar and listened to the British Forces Radio; on this particular night records were played during the evening and into the early hours for a blind children's charity; the idea was phone in for the record you wanted played, then it would go out to other units for tender and a bidding war would take place, units slowly dropping out along the way. The winning bid would have the record played in their name; one before midnight and one after. I can't remember the record played on New Year's Eve 1973 but have been reliably informed by Chris (Benny) Dearne that we bid second place for Mario Lanza's 'The Drinking Song'; perhaps as we came second we didn't have to pay anything.

In his own words - *(Chris Benny Dearne RE - I was one of the Barman at the time, whatever you did or did not do you got a fine towards BFBS for the poor little blind boys, we got 2nd place for the old year's song, the drinking song by Mario Lanzo! A great but very drunk Christmas!)* Thanks Chris... *Just to clarify before the PC brigade kick in; the money went to girls as well.*

What I do remember is sitting at the bar with Reg Reid and Kev Steward singing Dean Martin numbers on the top of our voices. This was the start of a good friendship. On return from Northern Ireland in November the following year a new MT troop would be formed and Kev, Reg and I would end up living in adjacent rooms in the HQ and MT lines. The three of us would become good mates and work together for over two years.

Prior to Op Banner we had an HQ troop but no MT troop the Field troops drivers were part of the troop they worked with; it's debatable which system worked best.

FFR (Fit For Role) January 1974

The next day 1st January 1974 was a Bank Holiday and a slow start for most of us. Nothing was open including the garrison cinemas. I prepared my kit, done some dhobi and wrote some letters. This year would be a monumentous year for me; I would be involved in military tasks that would, over the space of four months in Northern Ireland turn me from a boy who thought he was a man into the real thing. I would be witness to extreme violence, see carnage and human tragedy; I would be shot at, blown up and come close on a few occasions to losing my life in an active service role. So bring it on - Operation Banner, Ballykelly and all the stuff leading up to our deployment.

The 2nd January 1974 was a Wednesday and we paraded as normal at 0820. Our Troop commanders informed us the OC would address us at 1330 after lunch; we would form up in troops and march to the gym.

Following lunch we quickly fell-in; it was sleeting and cold. 1 Troop on the left of the parade was called up by Fred Ludlow, left-turned and marched the 100 yards to the gym door, the three other Troops following. Eventually we were all inside, the whole Squadron, in three ranks across the width of the gym where large dust sheets had been laid on the wood flooring. Bill Dunn came in carrying a step-up which he placed on the floor in front of us; he then addressed us...

'When the OC comes in I will call you up; slide - I repeat, slide your foot across to the attention, DO NOT stamp; we want to keep the gym floor in one piece. Listen in to what the OC tells you.'

Within a couple of minutes the OC came through the door.

'Squadron, Squadron SHUN!' Gave out Bill.

We slid smartly to attention.

The OC mounted the step-up placed before us.

'Right men, gather round and stand easy.' We shuffled into semi-circle in front of the Boss.

'First chaps, on behalf of the officers and Senior NCOs let me wish you all a happy new year. I hope it will be successful year for all of us as a Squadron and as individuals. Although there has been no official announcement you are all by now aware we are deploying later this year to Northern Ireland as a Squadron in an Engineer role. The location, for those of you not yet aware and I'm sure there are none; is Ballykelly airfield outside of Londonderry, the airfield is no longer operational in the flying sense but is home to a number of different army units. This will not be an easy deployment; tensions in the province are running very high. Internment without trial is proving to be a major bone of contention and a driving force for violence. I do not see this tour as anything but difficult. So we will begin our preparations from now. The physical fitness of the Squadron which I'm informed is not where it should be will be improved tenfold; we are fortunate to have two very able Regimental PTIs in the Squadron - Corporal Bell and Sapper Eastwood who will take great pleasure I'm sure in assisting you all on the road to physical perfection. (A general laugh from us all).'

The two Pete's - Pete Bell and Pete Eastwood were both super-fit; Pete Bell had been with the Squadron for some time, was a boxer of the highest calibre and loved, like all PTIs showing off his fitness and putting his compadere's through their paces. Pete Eastwood on the other hand was an unknown quality to anyone other than Taff Graham and me. Pete had been in our Junior intake and progressed through Dover with us passing out a term before us. Even at Dover he was fitness crazy and led the field in almost everything involving stamina. He'd been a part of my Course 7 at Dover had completed in the British Legion March and Shoot competition and was in the same section as me winning the assault course competition. I believe I'm correct in saying the first thing he applied for on arriving at Sixteen the previous July was a Regimental PTI course to which he was accepted and excelled. Pete was a dead on guy until you had to do physical training under him… then LOOK OUT! He like all PTIs grew horns.
The OC continued…

'We will start with road-runs in the morning at 0730, we'll run our regular two mile route across the road and through the quarry.

These runs will include all personnel not involved with other duties. We will continue with sport on a Wednesday afternoon and following FFR inspection at the end of this month I will introduce a five mile run on Friday afternoons; we'll undertake night route marches in full battle order with weapon.

As deployment moves closer more time will be spent training in Sennelager at Tin City; most of you will be familiar with the training establishment having spent time on its construction. The training will replicate what you may expect on the streets of Londonderry.

Our Engineer role will also include a further role aside from the normal construction work. We will be training three sections - one from each troop in IED search; for those of you not familiar with the term IED it means Improvised Explosive Device. The Provo's are becoming very advanced in the use of the bobby trap; their differing types and methods of initiation. Consequently the army need far greater in-depth training to find them, recognise them and counter them. In short they need specialist search teams trained in that role; those first teams will be provided by us Engineers. The course will be the first of its kind with 33 Squadron based in Antrim and ourselves providing the first teams. It will be held at the RE bomb disposal school at Chattenden. Volunteers will be sought at a later date. Returning to the subject of FFR - fitness for role; This is a Regimental inspection with all Squadrons taking part including Four Three Field Support and RHQ; preparation will continue through this month with the inspection taking place by armed forces auditors on the 29th, 30th and 31st of January. All our vehicles and equipment will be inspected for cleanliness and worthiness as will the block and everything in it. That will be day one and two. It is quite likely that the Regiment will be asked to deploy to Achmer on day three and adopt tactical defensive positions as we would should those real life circumstance present themselves. For this coming inspection all broken and worn parts need to be replaced wherever possible. I know how difficult it is to obtain replacement anything but we must do our best; I'm sure it'll be one hundred percent on the day. Thank you Gentlemen we will further brief you on Operation Banner closer to the time. Please pose any question through your troop commanders - Sergeant Major?'

'Nothing to add Sir.'

'Excellent, carry on please.'

'Squadron – Squadron - SHUN!' Once more we came to attention as the OC and our officer group left the gym.

'RIGHT! Listen in.' Commanded the SSM. 'Squadron stand at EASE! – stand easy. These are early days. For the next month we will be concentrating on FFR. For those living in the block we will be conducting room and line inspections. The days these inspections take place will appear on Part 2 orders and all personnel that do not live-in will not – I repeat will not, enter the lines on those mornings. That's all men; troop NCOs carry on.'

The SSM along with other SNCOs left the gym and slowly in chattering groups we formed up in small squads and left for our places of work.

Orders that evening contained most of what the OC had told us. It informed us that physical training in the form of gym work and running which would begin the following week. It also contained another pre-warning. A CPX would take place for five days during the second week in February. Those involved would be informed. I mentioned earlier command post exercises involved HQ elements from company or in the case of Engineer units, Squadrons; up to Brigade level.

16, along with 37, 12 and 39 Field Squadrons, 31 Armoured RE Squadron and 43 Field Support Squadron made up 2 Division RE part of the 12th Mechanised Brigade. In 1976 23 and 25 Engineer Regiments would amalgamate to form 2 Armoured Division Engineer Regiment. In this process (as with all reshuffles for cost saving) inevitably one Field Squadron would be lost; that would be 37. These changes wouldn't last long either with another reformation coming less than half a decade later. It would take the arrival of a new Conservative Government under a first female Prime Minister to go some way to rebuilding the five years of damage to numbers and morale implemented under the labour administration.

Monday 7th January was the first room inspection; Fred Ludlow came through 1 Troop lines with Timmy Wray, it wasn't necessarily the cleanliness they were looking for it was also the general condition of items within the room; bins that were stained and dented, chairs with seat backs broken, tables with damage to laminate tops, walls where sellotape had pulled off the paint. In the bathrooms cracked tiles, missing bath plugs and broken mirrors. All this stuff had to be repaired or replaced. We were told that on the inspection day all extras in the room had to put away in lockers... such as our brew kit, mugs, tins of bicies, radios that had the FM antenna lead taped to the wall. The washing machine in the bog was debatable. Tim needed to get guidance from higher up. Although it was pointed out to him that we bloody live here and our lives - singlies life's that is, were being disrupted and intruded aplenty; whereas the ffin pads were untroubled in their married quarters; no one went there and inspected every aspect of their living accommodation.

The washing machine ended up staying and unlikely as it sounds so did our wall mounted pin-ups. Probably because taking them down would have meant a complete room repaint. Any rooms with carpet that was unofficial (that's all of it) had to hide it; basically that would have been in the loft. Most carpeting had been nicked or cadged from somewhere or someone.

The corridors were a prize pain – the floor tiles were smooth around the edges in a kind of terracotta colour but down the centre they were ribbed and a real bastard to clean with a mop.

Above us in the loft the bar would be made spick-n-span prior to the inspection and would be locked until it was all over. Drinking would be done in the NAAFI bar. Below us the G1098 stores, signals store and other empty cellar rooms needed to be gone through in the same cleaning process.

On mornings of no inspection we were out either road-running or circuit training in the gym. 1 and 2 troops would run while 3 and HQ troop would gym; the next day we'd change over. We'd run out the gate swing left along the back of our block on 'An den Netter Heide' and cross the road into a large wooded reserve, we were now 400 yards into our run and guys would be honking-up the previous night's beer or recently consumed fried breakfast into the gutter. We never learnt; the same thing would happen every morning.

The days we were in the gym were no easier. Press-ups, sit-ups, medicine ball, bunny hops, even climbing the bloody rope! All under the watchful eye of Messer's Eastwood and Bell.

At the MT it was all out war; vehicles were not only cleaned they were painted as well. Taff Baines was the paint sprayer delegate; with an airline and two pots – one of matt black and one of a pond algae green, with a pile of cardboard window cut-outs he ploughed through the vehicles one after the other with one assistant holding the cardboard over lights and windows while another followed behind with 2 jam-jars touching up around the areas the spray

Looking out of the window of my first room in 1 Tp lines 16 Flds Sqn; back off the block. The sports field across the road with our cross country course running up into the woodland behind.

gun couldn't reach and filling in the misses; real rough and ready stuff. Of course Merv was fully kitted out with PPE when doing this job wasn't he? Like hell he was, an old pair of green overalls replaced his good pair and that was it. Respiratory protection? Ha! You're having a laugh – an old cam-scarf tied around the nose and mouth was about it. Following the respraying all the Tac-marks had to be replaced, it was a hell of an undertaking, mud and other crap needed to be removed first, so just getting all the track and wheeled vehicles ready for spraying was a nightmare job in itself. Across from our garages the open wash-down area had three sets of massive concrete ramps and a small brick building containing a high pressure pump system; the ramps allowed tracked and wheeled wagons to be driven up and the undersides pressure washed... that's if you could a/ find the key to the pump room, b/ the pump was working, or c/ if you could hunt down the hoses and lances'. Most guys wanting to use this wash-down facility would give up in frustration and just grab a bucket and a brush. I remember using it once in four years.

The Regiment would be inspected on the day fully kitted out for tactical deployment. We'd be presented in Squadrons on the square and take whatever the auditing officers threw at us.

FFR inspection Jan 74; or possibly line up pre FTX. Photo TM.

The day of reckoning came; we were up early preparing the block. The inspecting officers would spend the day auditing HQ, 43 and the two Field Squadron accommodation stores and offices. We – the living-in guys were basically told to keep out of the way until it was over. The following day would be the inspection of RHQ while at the same time all the Regiments vehicles would line up on the square; presented as for deployment in the field. That took care of the 29th and 30th; the big question was would we be told to deploy to Achmer for inspection under tactical conditions. The answer would be yes.

Early on the morning of the 30th saw all drivers and APC commanders at the MT firing up their wagons and driving them round and into position on the square; vehicle access was on the opposite side of the square to Sixteen's block directly outside the NAAFI. Vehicles would be positioned in front of their respective Squadrons with the HQ transport element in front of RHQ. The day was freezing and some of those vehicles left outside proved a bastard to start. Merv's water browser refused point blank to start no matter what abuse he threw at it. It ended up being towed into position.

'Let's fucking hope they don't ask me to start it.' Was his only comment.

Scotty was flapping around like an old woman getting under everyone's feet. The general feeling was why doesn't stay in office and leave us to get on with it...

The whole regiment including 43 on parade was an impressive sight: Although we'd be in extended formation around the square prior to FTX in October 1975 we wouldn't line up in block formation again until the disbandment of 23 and 25 Engineer Regiments for the formation of 2 Division Armd Eng Regt in the late summer of 1976.

JNCOs were checking their sections and APCs; Troop SNCOs were checking those who were checking and Officers were milling around (normal practice) on the side lines. It all looked pretty good from where I was standing with my 1 Troop Bedford RL.

Slowly everyone was positioned correctly for the inspection. At 0930 Bill Dunn addressed us.

'Listen in Gentlemen. As the inspection team approaches the Squadron I will call you up. I will then stand you easy. As the inspecting officer approaches your vehicle you'll come to attention or in the case of section vehicles your section NCO will call you up. You may be spoken to or questioned by the inspecting officer as to your role. Please try to give a sensible answer... not 'I'm not sure Sir, or I'm here for my holidays, my lumbago or my missus kicked me out'. If all else fails you tell him you're here to stop the Russians.' *This caused a laugh from everyone.*

The inspection team split into groups starting with the RHQ element and 43 Squadron before inspecting us and moving on to 37 Squadron; those poor sods had quite a wait. However the whole circus moved on quite rapidly... for which there was a reason. The whisper moved through the ranks quite rapidly 'They're deploying us to Achmer'; us being the entire Regiment.

The inspection team moved off and we were briefed on what would happen prior to leaving the square.

Deployment, would take place in exactly the same way as it would if we were on high alert and received the order to deploy; not an uncommon situation in BAOR in the seventies.

In the early hours of the following morning under cover of darkness we would leave the barracks for the harbour area; the inspection team would drive out and inspect us within a deployed scenario. The only difference being we'd go ten miles up the road to Achmer rather than to our normal area of operation near Kassel.

The vehicles would remain on the square and during the day further kit and equipment would be loaded.

The major fly in the ointment I was to find out was that married personnel were allowed home to bed and trucks would be sent to collect them in the early hours of the morning.

This collecting of the Pads was a big gripe with the singlies. The living in drivers plus a mate had to be up and out driving round the Pads quarters knocking on doors at God knows what hour to bring the married guys into barracks. In many cases you'd be almost knocking the fucking door off its hinges before the bloke concerned opened it. I've even had some guy's wife (who'll remain nameless Barry Mills) who came to the door and asked me in a broad Northern Irish accent what the hell I wanted at such a god-forsaken hour. Sapper bloody Mills hadn't even told his wife we were in alert status and that it was highly likely he'd be on a shout...

During the mid-seventies there were around 70,000 British forces stationed in BAOR and I'm pretty certain this figure did not include those in Berlin who were considered dead and buried in the event of hostilities kicking-off.

Many were married with children; I've read a figure of 100,000 during the nineteen seventies for civilian women and children alone. The pre-warning and deployment to our operational area time-line in the event of an Eastern Bloc attack was 48 hours. So in 48 hours we had to have loaded, collected all our personnel and deployed tactically to our positions near Kassel. This would be status RED. Prior to Red we should (technically if the Reds were playing fair) already be in Amber, trucks loaded radios on board, cam-nets and poles strapped down and personal kit at a point where you could grab it and run... run toward the forthcoming war that is, not away from it.

The big unknown was how would the real thing affect the married personnel? Nobody knew how a married soldier or airman would behave when he (or she) was leaving their quarter, their wife, kids and belongings, almost certainly for the last time.

The big plan was that their families and thousands of other families would be rounded up and moved westward to the coast, but this exercise was never tried or tested. It was a colossal logistical undertaking which in reality was not practical or sustainable.

How? How on earth could you move that many people? Who would move them? The German police would be looking after their own population; probably moving them back from the border area in fleets of buses mustered from all over the country. The British Military police would be directing troops to the front and keeping routes clear. There would just not be the resources to evacuate British families... and then you have a small percentage of Squaddies that are married to, or living with, German girls. They'd probably go nowhere, wanting to stay with their German family rather than be moved back to the UK. How would an advancing army, an army whose sole objective is to take over the North Sea and channel coastal ports in the shortest possible time deal with the families of British and American service personnel. Crush them underfoot or track? Round them up and use them as living hostages? It really was an unknown factor.

The emotional conflict of interest for the married soldier would in the event of hostilities be extremely great. I defy any man or women to walk out of the door not knowing what was going to happen to their family. My assessment was, while out rounding up the pads that night, that in the event of a real war many would put their families first and wouldn't turn up until they knew they were safely on the route back to Blighty. In fact I've even heard that scenario voiced by some guys over a beer. I was seventeen years old but astute enough to know that practice and train as hard and as much as we could, if the shit hit the fan it would be one big disorganised almighty fuck-up. I shall return to the disorganised element of my statement later.

It was hardly worth going to bed; the 'Pad-run' began at 0130 with a whole bunch of us live-in drivers heading for the MT, not just drivers but another bod with you to help with the door banging. We had the addresses of all personnel that needed knocking up and the married quarters to which we'd been allocated; dozens of trucks poured out of Roberts heading for all the different quarters; not just Sixteen Squadrons but the other Squadrons as well.

By 0430 after a painful collection, every Pad had been rounded up and we're fired up ready to roll.

I'd heard the expression a few times since I'd arrived at Sixteen; 'Whinging Pads'; now having done this midnight run to get them out of bed I knew exactly what the expression meant. Talk about bloody moan... woke up the missus, woke up the dog, knocked to loudly and set off the kids, why pick me up before him? You could have rang ahead... as if! God almighty!

Finally with the OC next to him, Red McCracken led 16 Squadron contingent of the Regiment in our freshly painted and spotlessly clean battle wagons out the gates and left toward Achmer.

The Achmer training area was (*I say was because I believe it's now been returned to the German people and a great deal of change has taken place*), a large tract of woodland and heathland

which covered an area fifteen klicks to the north west of Osnabruck in a triangle roughly between three little villages - Bramche in the east, Ufflen in the north, on a direct line to Hollage at the southern end. Although heavily wooded in places the area was severely churned up due to the tracked and other heavy vehicles that used it from the Osnabruck garrison.

We would head out of town on Furstenauer Weg toward Hollage and take one of the forested tracks off the road into the training area. This was just one of many entry points to numerous different parts of the heath.

On the morning of the 31st January the whole Regiment was on the move and I have to admit driving along with Cobby in my RL I was well impressed.

Through Hollage and onto one of the small backroads we suddenly swung to the right onto a very muddy track; all lights went out, although it was now 05.30 it was middle of winter and still pitch black. I engaged the four wheel drive.

'Switch to convoy light Steve,' said Cobby; I guess he was keeping a wary eye on me as the Sprog driver of the troop. I done as he said and peered ahead through the minuscule windscreen at the small light at ground level which was Fred Ludlow's Ferret scout car in front of me.

Although I'd spent more than a day training in cross country driving with Merv, back in early December, this morning, in the dark, was a whole different ball game. Just trying to avoid getting to far behind Fred and losing my way terrified me, I'd never live it down. Also I didn't want to get to close and run into the back of him. My concentration was total, at times it seemed we were driving through puddles three foot deep, the truck bucked one way and then the other; I could feel the wheels spinning beneath me and the steering wheel roughly 24" in diameter had a mind of its own, there must have been enough play in the steering gear and ball joints to slide a pencil between. Water sloshed around the wheels and every now and again Cobby would offer a sentence of advice, he'd been here a dozen times before – not here as in location but here as in situation.

When we'd started out an hour before, the cab had been freezing, Cobby had lifted the engine cowl to get some warmth in the cap but not now, I was sweating buckets and had the window wide open to prevent the screen from misting up. Through the open window I could hear the engines of the Troop APCs making their distinctive high pitched engine noise, any Field Troop Sapper who's travelled in the back of one of these cramped and almost claustrophobic war wagons will read this and remember the engine whine. With only two hatches one for the commander and one for the driver, (who, even with parka, cam-scarf's and cap comforters wrapped round the face, froze in the ice cold air), the rest of the section just jammed themselves together below, rolling with the vehicle motion with no clue to where they were going or what was going to happen next; they could have dropped off the side of a cliff and been totally unaware it was going to happen. Two years up the road on Exercise in Fort Carson Colorado I would see this actually happen, it was a grim experience.

In my four years in BAOR I never travelled in the back of an APC and I'm eternally grateful I never had to, I'm a bloke who likes to be in control of the vehicle he's in, or at least know what's going

on around me. A combat engineer Sapper in the back of an APC...
no thanks.

After what seemed like eternity we came to a halt. Fred
wrapped on the cab door and Cobby stuck his head out.

'Stay here Gordon, the sections are pulling in under cover.
We'll get them in position and then pull you guys in a spot to set up
the kitchen. Turn the engine off Burt.'

We sat in silence for a few minutes other than the crunch of
vegetation and the whine of the APCs manoeuvring in under the
tree canopy. Fred appeared again. 'Gordon come with me.' Gordon
opened the door and jumped out. Within minutes he was back.

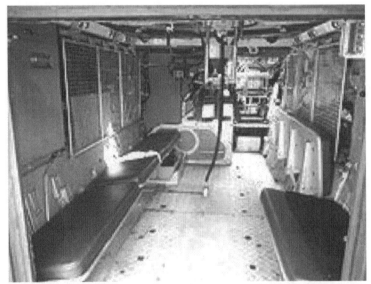

Steve get out here, I'll show you where were harbouring-up.'

The sky was just beginning to pale, I could make out the
whole troop harboured up in a circle over a couple of hundred
yards each section busily engaged in dragging their canvas and
cam-nets over the long poles they carried tied down between the
top boxes.

Cobby showed me where he was going to back me in. 'Watch
me Steve - left hand out-stretched is right hand down and vice-
versa if I drop my arm you go back as you are, ok?'

'Yeah I'm with you,' I replied. I noticed the poor cook was out
of the back and standing to one side.

Slowly after some toing-and-froing we got the wagon positioned.

Before we began camming-up the tail-gate was dropped and the hydro-burner and hot plate taken down – a Dixie filled with water and we left the cook to get a brew on for the lads. Breakfast would follow.

(The Hydro-burner - Introduced in 1939 the Cooker No.1 or Hydro burner as it was known became standard equipment for the next 40 years until health and safety ruled them unsafe for use. (Crap, they were as safe as... well as safe as the bloke using it).

Consisting of a 2 gallon petrol tank pressurised by a foot or built in hand pump, it fired a jet of flame along a trench covered by a hinged metal plate about four foot long with three big holes in the top. The plate and holes accommodated three large Dixie's. The end could either be plated off or have another Dixie stood hard up against it). The photo to the right shows the burner, plates, Dixie's and a Haybox – the Haybox being an oversize thermos.

Gordon and I dragged the poles from where they were held down under the cam-nets that were already hooked in place over the top of the truck canopy - two of them.

Camming-up is a bit of an art form; it's not that easy, you need to break up the silhouette of the vehicle, by suspending the net above it. But like everything else it comes with practice and you find a method that works for you or your section, everyone has their job.

The APCs carried a large canvas that they put over the top boxes as a tent before unrolling the net. If they didn't do this the net would catch on every metal protrusion on the hull. A nightmare if you were trying to do this in the dark. The canvas tent also provided a sleeping area. Within the top of the APC was a large rectangular hatch roughly at a guess six foot by four; this hatch would open outwards in two halves and fold back. The section guys would open one side and sleep two on the top, two on the floor and four on the bench seats.

For Cobby the cook and I the clock was ticking, when the Troop had cammed-up they'd be ready for food and it was our job to help the cook prepare it.

Hydro-burner and Dixie-plate were in position and water was on for a brew. We had a kind of green gazebo that we erected over the cook area which also needed to be cammed-up. When I looked at it I wondered if the Ruskies done the same thing...? Although everything was covered with nets it all looked a bit medieval in appearance and vulnerable to attack. Slowly the guys wandered over and stood around waiting for the water to boil; each man wore webbing, carried a SLR or SMG and had his Noddy suit on his belt – around thirty five of us in all.

Fred and Timmy stepped forward to brief us...

Fred began. 'Right lads, listen in. When the inspection team gets here and I doubt that will be for a couple of hours we'll be in stand-to, until then we'll remain tactical, sentry's will be posted, the crap pit dug, anyone not engaged in anything useful stay in your wagon.

(*For anyone who doesn't know what Stand-to is its short for 'Stand-to-Arms', the process of Stand-To was observed morning and evening by both sides most notably on the Western Front; the war in the trenches.*

Each man would be expected to stand on the trench fire step, rifle loaded, bayonet fixed. The theory ran that most enemy attacks were mounted either before dawn or shortly after dusk under cover of darkness. Consequently both sides took care to ensure adequate preparation at such times, manning the fire step an hour before dawn and dusk.

There was an obvious irony in that both sides took such elaborate precautions against the eventuality of an attack despite the fact that each would be engaged in Stand-To at exactly the same time. Nevertheless attacks were indeed launched at either dawn or dusk, particularly once it became clear to one side that the trench opposite was manned by relatively inexperienced troops.

Both sides would often relieve the tension of the early hours with machine gun fire, shelling and small arms fire, directed into the mist to their front: this made doubly sure of safety at dawn.

'Stand-To' lasted between half an hour and an hour. The whispered word would go out, 'Stand-To' and we would silently move out into our pre-allocated perimeter positions; after which each man would be ordered quietly to 'Stand-Down'; breakfast would follow in the morning.

What I didn't get was — if both sides knew that each other Stood-To at the same time, then Stood-Down at the same time, how come one side didn't wait until the other side Stood-Down and either went to sleep or had breakfast and then attacked? I suppose it had been proved to work, I still thought it was a bit of a waste of time; but then I was just a lowly Sapper...

They'll inspect what they want to and hopefully sign us off as job done. We'll then de-cam, clear up and return to Roberts. The immediate job is to allocate Stand-to positions, then breakfast... Ok, one-one-Alpha come with me other sections return to your wagons.'

Paddy Holmes and his section went off with Fred while the other guys formed a queue for a brew and went back to their section APCs to wait the call Stand-to positions and scoff.

When a Troop was harboured up together the central kitchen churned out the food. If the sections were working individually on tasks they catered for themselves from the ten man ration packs. The troop hadn't brought a great deal of food, a half dozen ten man Compo packs, bread and trays of fresh eggs, enough for breakfast and lunch. I started emptying tins of tomatoes into a

114

Dixie; Cobby prepared the brew while the cook dug out a huge frying pan and oil for the eggs and spam fritters. These fritters were a kind of luncheon-meat as my gran would call it, the posh name for spam, in tins that could be sliced and ate cold, put in a stew, or fried. I'd eaten it before at Dover and really quite liked it.

Water boiled, the lads queued for a brew, probably the most important thing for moral. They took their drinks back to the wagon and waited breakfast call.

All three of us worked on the food and when it was ready we gave the lads a shout, it was 0800 now and light; everyone other than the cook had been shown their Stand-to position. A second Dixie was on the plate for brew water and hot water to clean mess tins and Dixie's. Cobby, the cook, and I had retired to eat our own scoff sitting on water Jerry cans and Compo boxes in the shelter of the lean-to. Timmy Wray, Fred and their two drivers Barry Mills and Alfie Doyle were also in there, how Alfie ever got through the hatch of a Ferret Scout Car I'll never know, he wasn't really built for it... As we sat there eating and talking it started to snow.

'Look at that,' I said. That's all we bloody well need.'

'Welcome to the cold war Stevie. You didn't know what you were letting yourself in for when you picked a Field Squadron in Germany did you? You got three years of this sunshine, better get used to it. Great fun isn't it Cobby?'

'Oh yeah a bundle of laughs, replied Gordon.' This was Alfie Doyle talking; all the rest were grinning; including Fred and Timmy Wray. (Who sadly would never get to take his Troop on an FTX).

By dusk we'd returned to Roberts; our gleaming vehicles which had looked spotless on the square the previous day were caked in mud.

We had been the last Squadron to be audited in the field and to top it off they arrived just as the corn-dog hash was ready for serving at lunch.

The guard had stopped the convoy on our perimeter and the escorting officer had demanded our sentry shout Stand-to while at the same time blow his whistle for a gas attack. We were running for the trees while at the same time trying to don our Noddy-suits – the bastards. Still, twenty minutes later they'd gone and we were scoffing and rolling up the cam nets.

All the gear chucked into the back of the wagon, in convoy with Timmy out front we rolled back to Traz. (Osnabruck was nick-named Osnatraz by the troops stationed there; this name was abbreviated to Traz).

Part 2 orders that Thursday evening, stated that there would be no parade on the Friday. Duties would commence at 0830 which involved unloading all the exercise kit back into the stores and cleaning vehicles. Knock-off would be lunch time.

This had been my first taster of how things worked in the field; how I, as a Troop G10 wagon driver would fulfil my duties alongside the Troop storeman and the cook. I'd quickly decided a G10 driver was not going to be a long term occupation for me' I'd never peeled so many sodding spuds!

Deirdre and the armoured 'Pig'

FFR over we were now free to have a mega piss-up before starting the serious training leading up to Ballykelly.

It was also the beginning of February, with a week of carnival and the Rosenmontag celebrations; a very big deal in north Germany and the Rhineland area.

Rumour had it that parties of women would be out celebrating ladies day, getting drunk and grabbing men in the street? Yeah right... However there was a very raucous week ahead with parades, a funfair and of course lots of drinking and late nights. The German carnival season ends at the start of 'Lent'.

That night we all hit town; a few beers in the Winkle and then taxi's to the Scratch. This was my first time in the disco which was then located on one of the busy streets in the old town; the building is still there; it's no longer a disco and the area has been pedestrianised whereas in 1974 the Monkey wagon could pull up directly outside the door disgorging its content of Red-caps into the fray.

The disco was on the second floor, you went through the front door up the stairs and the dance floor was in front of you with the bar area over to the right. Big plate glass windows looked out over the street below with soft seating underneath them. There were plenty of loose tables and chairs scattered around the place; the seating continued around the other side of a 'U' shaped bar. It was a large disco holding at a guess around 250 people. How can I describe the atmosphere... well it gave you the feeling that any second a brawl would break out and very often this was the case. It was a melting pot of young men from over a dozen different army units, all with massive egos; this also included the German civilians brave enough to frequent the place. There were of course girls and more mature women, German and English. It was not uncommon for Pads wives to frequent the Scratch if hubby was on exercise or over in Northern Ireland.

Coloured lights flashed over the ceiling while 'Mud' banged out Tiger Feet and 'Sweet' were on a Teenage Rampage. It was dark, noisy and manic with loads of people wearing party costumes and make-up. There were no seats vacant so a couple of us muscled our way to the bar and got a round in. We moved off to an area where we could watch what was going on... there wasn't much else to do; it was too noisy to hold a conversation, there was nowhere to put a glass down. There were no vacant seats, you could barely see anything, but maybe with a bit of luck we'd stumble upon some loose talent.

Wishful thinking indeed, we never even came close to a dance. After an hour of this, standing with a beer glass in my hand I was getting fed up, it wouldn't have been so bad if at least there were some seats but standing in one place watching other people gyrating on a dance floor has never been my strong point. The decision to move on to another bar was made for us when a bust up started, which within seconds had spread like a fire. There was a load of shouting and screaming, the lights came on and the music stopped but the punch-up continued. The bouncers ran up from the front doors but stood little chance of stopping the brawl. 'Come on,' said Titch, 'time to be moving on.' We got out of the place smartish and headed for a normal bar in the old town.

The fights in the Scratch were legendary; the German police would turn up with dogs, British and Bundeswehr MPs would turn up with batons. In italics below I've pasted a Facebook conversation revolving around the Scratch and our local Eros centre, Frank Butler kicks off...

Frank Butler - Remember it well! (The Scratch). Many a good night. When we left the Saskatchewan (impressed you there!) We went to a sit-down Chinese Restaurant can't remember the name. Then the Brothel for a look! A look? Yeah right Frank. (SB)

Stephen Hannon - Brothel on the corner then on to the Brocky stand outside the station.

Frank Butler - Wasn't it called the Eros Centre?

Steve Burt - Yes you could be right... part of a government franchise :)

Baz Gazey - The Sasquatch. Remember being at the top of those wide stairs when the dogs came in. Big Dobie staring me out.

Eros centre was a state sponsored brothel and very useful to dive in on payday, grab a quickie for 10 bucks (30 Baz. SB) *then get around to the sasquatch and have a dance. Always enjoyed watching the squaddies trying to chat up the birds whilst buying em drinks that cost the earth. 10 bucks was cheap. Taff Baines used to go with his missus and dance the arse off everybody. I remember a restaurant underneath the club but rarely went in. Easier to flop into Pops or the schnelly round by the station. Appy days.*

Steve Burt - *Remember Bopper Bennett with his crape sole shoes and long velvet maroon coat Baz? He worked in the evenings on the door of the Eros centre. He was in the room next to us in MT lines. What a hoot!*

Baz Gazey - *I remember Bopper very well. Lovely bloke. Think he got a flat rate but also a BJ by the on duty howler. His motorcycle "trophies" were all hand painted and when he got on a Can-am, he promptly fell off.*

Steve Burt - *Thats right... forgotten about his motor bike mania, I was planning on buying a car and bringing it back to Traz he spent ages trying to convince me a bike was better. My argument was you can always shag a bit of totty in the back of a car when is raining. less fun over the saddle of a bike :)*

Stephen Hannon - *Anybody remember the lad who wanted to marry the bird who had the big brown Mercedes, if I remember she was one of the lady's of the night.*

Steve Burt - *Peanut Kent, 2Tp? She would visit the Squadron bar. When word got back to RHQ they had him on a plane in 24hrs - posted to Waterbeach. As soon as he got there he applied for leave and within 48 hrs was back in Traz. He did see her for ages before he got rumbled. She had a luxury apartment in the town. Good ole Peanut.*

Stephen Hannon - *That's it Steve, I remember him being marched to the nick before being flown out.*

Steve Burt - *Peanut was a head case; he went AWOL when we were in Colorado for a couple of days, shacked up with some doll. Paddy McIntyre went ballistic, he was confined to the block for the rest of the tour. Not that he took any notice. He also drove his APC* over the top of a car that was parked almost outside 25s RHQ, we were still 23 & 25 at that point.

Stephen Hannon - Yep remember the car didn't it belong to one of the local workers.

Steve Doogle Adkins – Me, Titch Maughan, Ginge Hodgson and Hamish Hamilton went to the Scratch on our first night in Traz January 74.

Somehow every time I went there I got into trouble it must of been because of my big ears. I saw a Para get thrown through the window.

I got out in 78 and stayed in Osnabruck and married a German girl divorced in 81 and worked as a DJ from 78 till 83 both at the Scratch and Sheune (Village) for big Hans and Rosie.

The Scratch changed names in 81 to Club 99, I was DJ and Manager from 81-83 after the owner Adolf sold it to Arno the car dealer, I lived in the flats next door to it with all the hookers. I came home to UK and never went back.

Stephen Hannon - Steve didn't the para get hit by one of those bloody big glass ash trays they had on the tables before he went out the window?

The para's went down town that night to show who was the toughest and found out it wasn't them.

Steve Doogle Adkins - That's right Stevie. The Chinkies attacked one night as well 20 of them came running up those stairs with broom handles and they still got pummelled.

Steve Burt - Jeez! I'm glad I didn't hang around with you lot!

So as you can see we were well behaved and a credit to the Squadron, Regiment and Corp.

We were into February now and Fred Ludlow asked if I'd done my half day 'Induction to Germany' course at the education block, I had to admit that I hadn't. He told me to get over to the education block and find out when a session was running and book myself on.

There was a free place the following week, 10.30 to 12.00 so I put my name down and told Tom Byrne I wouldn't be available for driving duties that morning. That evening I walked over to 43 Field Support and had a beer with Taddy in their Squadron bar, like ours it was built in the attic space. You had to be a bit careful drinking in another Squadrons bar, it was by invitation only. You couldn't go wandering in and just order a pint, you needed to be accompanied. Strangers turning up unannounced could find themselves drinking a pint of special. This was a half pint of the barman's piss kept in a pint glass in the fridge, unwelcome visitors on ordering a pint of lager would be presented by the grinning barman with said glass topped up with a half pint of lager. It was not uncommon for someone to get halfway down the glass before realizing the beer tasted a bit odd. I warily kept an eye on where my pint was coming from.

I asked Alan if he'd done the induction thing, he hadn't.

'I was told to do it when I got here,' he said. 'But no one's bothered me about it since so I've done fuck-all about it.'

I could see myself being the only one turning up for this German culture familiarization and I was probably the person who needed it least of all.

Alan told me they had a dance on the coming Friday, why didn't I come over? I said I'd think about it.

I finally, after much prompting, ended up going to the induction with Peanut Kent and a Pad, who I seem to remember as Paul 'Johno' Johnson, an exceptionally well turned out model Sapper and that is said in all seriousness. Peanut as I'm sure you guessed was not his Christian name but a nick-name. Peanut was just that, a prize nutcase. He was continually in trouble although nothing really serious... well that may be a bit of an understatement, he drove his APC over a car parked outside 25 Regiment RHQ completely squashing it. This was late in 1975 after we'd returned from Colorado. In his defence he said he thought the car had been dumped. (Outside 25 RHQ? Yes Peanut, of course it was dumped); it belonged to a German civilian. He'd also managed to land himself in trouble while we were out in Colorado working with the United States 'B' Coy 4th Engineer Battalion in Fort Carson. I'll get back to that story at some other point.

Peanut was a good looking kid a bit of a babe magnet he had that 'take me home and mother me' look about him which older women seemed to fall over themselves for. I didn't realise it at the time but I gave off the same vibes. Neither of us seemed to have problems getting the girls and we knew what to do when we got them.

So Peanut elected to join me at the 43 Squadron dance, escorted to the bar and presented as genuine guests by Taddy.

We were both on the lookout... well I suppose Alan was as well, for women on their own... although we didn't hold out a great deal of hope; remember this was a Squadron do, and most women were accompanied by their husbands. The only chance of a single woman was an outsider that had been invited through the Squadron, or got wind of it on the grapevine.

Although the dance was invitation only to Squaddies outside of 43, it was open house to any women who fancied turning up. And that's how I met Deirdre, a loose woman in more ways than one.

Deirdre was one of a duo that stood at the bar, drink in hand talking, both these lassie's were in their mid-twenties and both were lookers. Alan after signing us in had gone off to talk to his mates leaving Peanut and I to eye-up the talent on offer and we were getting glances.

I was a bit shy with the chat-up lines, a failing that would inhibit my pulling prowess for a while to come; but not Peanut, he was like a bantam cock in a farm yard full of hens and before I knew it we were in a foursome with the two lovelies asking the mundane chat up questions and laughing over... well everything and nothing really.

So what was Deirdre doing at the 43 Squadron dance? Was her hubby a member of the Squadron, or was she sister to a Squadron member? No, neither of the aforementioned. Deirdre's husband was a soldier, yes. He was based in Roberts? No... so he was not a Royal Engineer. Where was he? He was away on a course.

However while we were becoming more and more pelvicly familiar on the dance floor she did not tell me what the course was or where it was being held, only that he may, or may not be away for some time. That suited me down to the ground.

Dance over we returned to our table and continued with light conversation. What Squadron was I in; where did she work? She worked in the NAAFI stores and supply over the back, which is how she'd got wind of the dance. Deirdre's leg now had a mind of its own as it rubbed its way up my own leg under the table.

'I need some fresh air,' she said looking at me.

'Ok,' I said, don't be long...' she looked at me as if I was a brick short of a load before bending over and whispering in my ear – 'we both need fresh air Steve.' Then pulled me bodily from the chair. Ah, the penny dropped, and not before time.

Down the stairs, out of the block and round the back; 43 Squadron car parking area. Within sixty seconds of leaving the bar I was pinned to the wall between two cars with her body pressed against mine and her tongue trying to snare my tonsils; a heady mix of brandy and cigarettes on her breath made me weak at the knees. 'Cor' I thought, I can put up with this.

It was cold against the wall but I was warming up rapidly, we'd both left our coats upstairs but she was warmer than me with a heavy wool maxi skirt and boots, blouse and bolero type top. I was in shirt sleeves.

'I'm not doing it here,' she said.

I could see it all slipping away... not that I'd even contemplated doing it...

'No? Why not,' was my desperate, spontaneous and teeth chattering reply.

'Because it's too cold and to public, that's why.'

Well when can I see you again, how can we get in touch with each other, have you got a phone?' The questions, in desperation, tumbled out of me.

'Let's go back upstairs, I'm cold and you're shivering.' She said.

'No I'm ok, I'm ok, just a couple more minutes.' Cold or not this was too good to give up. She relaxed again into my arms and we carried on snogging while I managed to loosen a button on the blouse and warm a hand up.

'How old are you Steve?' She asked.

'Nineteen,' was my reply.

'God you fibber, I must be crazy,' she mumbled. I held on tighter...

When we eventually got back to the bar Peanut and partner had disappeared. She was a Scottish girl who lived in the same block as Deirdre and worked in the Pads NAAFI over by Woolwich Barracks. Her husband was in Ireland with one of the Jock Regiments. Peanut got a shag but never saw her again, he wasn't into commitment or anything that could backfire on him - sensible. He also said the accent was so bad it was like talking to a chain saw.

Deirdre bought us another drink and we sat and discussed how we'd meet; it would only be in the evenings, one or two nights a week. She had a phone and I'd call asking for Hazel. If she answered saying 'Sorry no Hazel here,' then I'd hang up. If all was ok she'd say hi Steve and normal conversation would resume.

We picked up our coats and in the melee of the party atmosphere left the dance unnoticed. I walked her as far as the end of the cookhouse where we could see a couple of cab lights on the pavement outside the main gate; I said goodnight and swung a left down to my block.

I went to bed wondering if she would have the bottle to meet me again.

Nobby was awake. 'You stink of perfume Steve; got lucky did you?'

'Maybe Nobby, maybe...'

We met within a couple of days at the Dodesheide cinema, this venue was on the exact opposite side of the town to Lotte, the area of Osnabruck where her quarter was situated. My new found pastime said it was less likely that someone would know her. It was all very clandestine; I was the first to arrive and waited in the foyer until Deirdre turned up, she looked 'drop dead gorgeous' wearing again her maxi skirt and boots covered with a long wool coat. One behind the other without speaking we got in the queue for tickets, once you had a ticket you could sit anywhere as there was no seat number allocation.

I followed her through into the seating area still not taking any interest and staying a couple of paces behind. She walked through the rows to the back, the furthest seating from the door. The lights were still on and I was very conscious of eyes on us. The film was 'The Sting' another Redford, Newman film that had only just been released. I was looking forward to it.

We took our seats as the lights dimmed and adverts began in English for local trades and restaurants in Osnabruck – a kind of British Forces Pearl & Dean.

I didn't waste any time; as soon as those lights had dimmed I was in there like a rat up a drain pipe. The maxi skirt was buttoned up the front and I wasted no time in separating button from button hole - no tights? Well there's preplanning for you. Probably the reason there was no objection from Deirdre who just slid lower in the seat and seemed to be throwing herself wholeheartedly into the festivities.

The adverts finished and the black screen appeared to tell us that Jo Bloggs had rated the film X, Y or Z. I untangled my digits from Deirdre's Frenchie's and laid back in my seat to start watching the movie.

'What's up?' She whispered leaning over me and talking into my ear...

'The films starting; you don't want to miss the beginning do you,' I replied.

'Oh?' (And that 'Oh' had a mix of meanings to it).

She sat up straight and started putting her clothing back together. When completed she grabbed my hand.

'Come on, we're leaving,' she hissed.

With a grip like a wrestler I had no option; I was practically dragged along behind her.

'But the film, what about the film,' I whispered as quietly but as urgently as I could. She'd let go of me by now and I was just following as people turned in their seats to look. Dodesheide cinema catered for all the quarters and barracks on the north side of the town, I was saying a silent prayer that there was none of my mates around to witness my departure with a rather delectable women obviously older than I. That would be round the bloody Squadron like wild-fire. Thing was the films in the military cinemas changed very regularly sometimes only showing for one night, so if you wanted to catch a film you had to get in quick and this particular film was a relatively new release.

As far as I was aware we got outside unobserved.

What's up,' I asked.

'I don't want to see the movie Steve. I'm going home and you're coming with me, what I've got planned is far more fun, let's make the most of our time together.'

The fact was she had a 'things to do' list and shagging was on it. I was expected to help her tick that particular box which was fine by me...

Taxi's were everywhere, in no time we were in a car and at her pad.

I really was putting my life on the line bonking this girl. Eventually she told me her husband was in Hereford on selection for 22 SAS. I'm sure if her old man ever found out, him and his mates would roast me slowly on a spit over an open fire on the Brecon's possibly sharing my balls as a starter.

I kept Deirdre and these meeting very quiet. I was over there almost every other night, screwing as if my life depended on it. After getting my kit ready, I'd take my coat and wander down to either the main gate or the Winkle where there was always a taxi or two waiting. It wasn't difficult in February and March as the evenings were still dark. I'd pay the taxi one way and Deirdre would pay the other.

It all came to an end one evening when the phone rang while I was at hers. It was her old man calling from Gutersloh; he was at the airfield getting the bus to Traz!

I sat up in bed in a state of panic listening to hubby telling her he'd be home in ninety minutes.

'What's that?' I asked. 'He's in Gutersloh!? Bloody hell, how the hell did that happen?'

'RTU'd,' she said (Returned to unit).' He got bounced this morning and on the plane this afternoon... you'd better get dressed and disappear Steve, I need to change the sheets, shower and try to get my head in gear.' I could see she was sad, yet needing to be practical; it was the end of a fling.

It was never going to be a long term thing, we both knew that.

'Don't worry we'll see each other around and who knows we may get another opportunity,' I said grinning.

I gave her a good snogging at the door and made my way to the Taxi rank. I thought I'd let things cool off a bit before contacting her.

I was off to the UK anyway, I'd be away for a couple of weeks with Tojo and Taff Baines doing a course on the Humber one ton armoured Pig.

Three drivers needed to be trained on this strange vehicle, that we were to find out not only resembled a Pig in appearance but handled like one as well. Apparently Pigs were on the vehicle itinerary at Ballykelly, therefore some of us needed to know how they worked and how to drive them. The Pigs were very rudimentary section vehicle, but they were armoured as opposed to the section long wheelbase Land Rovers which were only Makrolon (Polycarbonate) covered.

The Humber `Pig` was originally a stop-gap vehicle produced to provide the British army with an armoured personnel carrier. With the end of the Second World War, the British army had a number of obsolete Universal Carrier vehicles, which it either sold or scrapped, foolishly (as usual) before ordering a replacement vehicle. However, the Malaysian emergency in the late 1940`s showed that there was still a desperate need for an enclosed APC for the British Army. One result on the drawing board but not yet available was the Saracen APC.

The other, stop-gap introduced to fill the gap before Saracen availability, was the Humber Pig. The basic design is an armoured hull built on a standard truck chassis of the Humber 1 ton truck. It was apparently nicknamed the Pig for it's snout like front and it being a pig to drive.

By the book, there are two crew and six passengers carried. (An RE field section). Two rectangular firing ports are mounted in the side and there is a firing port in each of the rear doors. Its 4.5 litre 6 cylinder Rolls Royce B60 engine developed 120 brake horsepower and a speed of 45mph.

The Humber 1 ton or 'The Pig'.

By the late 1960`s, the Pigs were gradually being withdrawn from service, either mothballed, sold abroad or simply scrapped. Then came the `Troubles`. The rapidly deteriorating situation in Northern Ireland required a vehicle that could carry troops and police safely through areas where they could be exposed to hostile crowds throwing missiles or terrorist attack.

Some 500 `pigs` were brought back into service, many bought back from overseas. Throughout their new career, the pigs have been constantly upgraded to meet the new challenges that faced them.

A tail-board was added to stop bullets striking the feet of troops disembarking or sheltering behind the vehicle. Bull bars were added to the front, to push through barricades. The side stowage boxes were removed to prevent incendiaries and devices being placed inside. The versatile Pig proved relatively easy to adapt to its new role. However they hadn't bothered to upgrade the brakes!

Taff and Toj were both in HQ Troop. Their Troop Senior NCO was Scotty and their Troop Officer was the AO (Admin officer). It would have been logical to take the third driver for the Pig Course also from HQ Troop, but no it was me...

Once again I was called into the Troop office.

'The Humber one ton armoured Pig Burt, wheeled APC ever heard of it?' Questioned Timmy Wray. (My presentation from Dover was still fresh in my mind).

'Yes Sir, what would you like to know? I asked.

'Oh...' said Timmy, a bit taken back. 'You do do you, so give me some details.'

So I rattled off my knowledge, the statistics and history I'd meticulously researched for my Junior Cadre presentation in Dover; June 1972.

'Good,' he said when I'd expended my recital. 'You're an obvious candidate for a Course on the thing. You'll be joining Baines and Corporal Stevens; flying to UK on the eighth March, that's Friday next week, you report to Bordon on Sunday tenth.

If you want to go home for the Saturday you'll need to buy your own ticket from London. Rail warrant will be provided London to Liphook return. You call the Bordon guard room from Liphook and they'll come and get you. It's a week's course, you'll enjoy it, I've heard good reports about your driving from Staff Scott. Dismissed Burt, go and check in with the Chief, liaise with Baines and Corporal Stevens.

Job done then, it's nice to be consulted...

During the Deirdre period military life had continued...

As well as my daily driving duties, I'd attended the BAOR induction at the education wing along with a dozen others; which was in fact quite interesting, we'd been told about German customs, how we should behave, being careful not to catch the clap or divulge secrets to loose women who may be working for the Ruskies. Along with this 'life in Germany' lecture we were also given an insight into just what was ranged against us in the way of

Eastern Bloc Forces. Enough to turn your hair grey and have the blood run to your feet. The officer rounded-up the lecture...

'Gentleman; you are a part of the defence of the free-west. The north – south, Soviet, free-west border stretches thirteen hundred plus kilometres and was labelled by Winston Churchill during a speech in the USA in 1946 the 'Iron Curtain'. The name has stuck. In 1945 the west was conned. The western powers of the time believed that the division of Germany by the Soviets was temporary. The Soviets built a fence and then in 1963 over a brief weekend they divided Berlin. The West gentlemen, did not have the 'will' at the time to stop them, and we now reap what we sow.

In places the border is up to two kilometres in depth, it has 3.2 metre high chain link fence with automatic firing devices and anti-personnel mines scattered at a rate of three thousand for every kilometre. If that isn't enough to deter a would-be escapee there is an anti-vehicle ditch bordered by a ploughed and harrowed strip 6 metres deep. This strip is criss-crossed by wires that automatically activate more anti-personnel mines. There are hundreds of observation towers and patrols, which are carried out in twos. You would think that two guys together may get pally and aid each other in an escape? Yes, that would seem possible except each pair consist of at least one married soldier with children and many are KGB in standard border guard uniforms.

Putting forward an idea to run would be a very very risky business, your oppo would report you; one because he is KGB, two because the soldiers family would suffer in more ways than one, probably end up in the Gulag. As you can see Gentlemen a person needs to be very desperate to attempt an escape... but they do and many get killed in the process. It is Gentlemen a very harsh regime and I suggest you don't plan an escapade to try and get in; if you didn't get killed in the process you probably wouldn't get back.

In the few areas where there is no fence there are yellow markers and the guards can be quite close. Drunken Allied soldiers have crossed the line; they wished they hadn't. However there is an element of the population that they are only too willing to send us and that's the elderly... if an elderly person wants to come west they seem to have no problem getting permission to do so. Think about it; there is a glaringly obvious reason for that... yes money. The elderly cost money to take care of and provide nothing for the state in return; so give them to the west to feed and look after. Another indication of just how ruthless this regime is.

So who's ranged against us? Well to start with there are 50,000 East German border guards broken down into three commands north, centre and south. Central command is solely responsible for Berlin.

Taking into account conventional forces alone the Eastern Bloc can throw a massive army, or should I say armies against north Germany. We, 1BR have to contend with the group of Soviet forces Germany known as GSFG, the Soviet northern group of forces in Poland, Moscow and Belorussian military districts which are supported by the East Germans and Polish armies.

I'll repeat what I just said gents - that is against north Germany alone. There are armies further north to assault the Baltic States and armies further south to take central and south Germany, Austria and Italy. In East Germany alone the soviets have ten tank divisions and 16 motor rifle divisions. These are the numbers we are very likely to have thrown against us on our short sixty five kilometre front; the front that is 1BR Corp: 7,000 tanks, 5,000 APCs, 1,500 combat and transport aircraft and 400,000 combat troops. Without spoiling your day further I'd just like to add that this is probably just the first wave attack; there are plenty more in reserve. However on a brighter note (we *were all deathly quiet listening to this doom laden lecture)* we know we have a far greater advantage in training and equipment quality. We have the Gazelle attack helicopter, the A10 tank buster. We have far better communications and leadership. We know we're outnumbered in tanks eleven to one *(eleven to one! He's bloody optimistic.)* but ours are far more advanced in range finding and fire power. We know the terrain, because we train over it constantly. I know it looks grim Gentlemen but we can hold them. The free west depends on us. Any questions?'

We were silent for a moment then Peanut put his hand up.

131

'Your name Sapper?'

'Kent Sir.'

'What is your question Kent?'

'At what point are we going to be told this is a 'No-duff' Sir? And more to the point at what point are the German civi's going to be told to get out of the sodding way. Am I going to be able to take my track-pads out at some point or do I go off to war with big lumps of rubber stuck between my tracks?'

We were all laughing, we'd all heard the stories of how German civilians surrounded the army units when they were on exercise and refused to let them move; I would have first-hand experience of this the following year on FTX. Also our tracked vehicles, APCs and Tanks were compelled to have big lumps of rubber fitted between each track link. This was to prevent the roads being ripped to shreds while we exercised, but they didn't do much to assist in cross country traction and would need to be removed in the event of hostiles and serious warfare. As a rough guess a 432APC had 30 foot of track per side, each link about a foot in length so approximately sixty pads per APC. They would wear down like tread on a standard tyre and then require changing. Track-pad changing was a full time occupation for the sections and a prize pain in the ass.

'Well Kent all I can say is there will be some warning prior to attack... how long have you been in BAOR Kent?'

'Roughly three months Sir.'

'Well Kent there are more than a few small things that require preparation before the Soviets could launch an attack. If - and this is an highly improbable 'if', an attack was to come without any warning at all... well to put it bluntly we'd probably be up shit creek without a paddle. However we know the Eastern Bloc conduct serious field exercises in October and November and we on this side of the border do the same thing. We let them know they won't take us by surprise. We're watching them closely at all other times. We – and that we includes the American, French and German armies as well as the Soviets monitor each other's exercises. These are done with... let's call them umpires in civilian vehicles. The cars have special number plates and they are allowed into certain areas of the exercise. However if you see one you can stop it, detain it, and call the Military Police who will escort them back to the border. Our registrations are called Brixmis and the Soviet's are called Soxmis. You cannot be heavy handed with these people; officially they are not the enemy, they are here by invitation or should I say agreement and their, our, presence goes some way to relieving tension and giving both sides of the border an indication of what is going on. This agreement may even prevent a catastrophic mistake taking place. So keep your eyes peeled for Soxmis registrations when you're out and about; on exercise or not.

'Thank you Sir, I appreciate your honesty.' Came tongue in cheek for Peanut.

'Well lads if there are no other questions you're free to go. I'd just like to add that we do run trips from here to the concentration camp Bergen Belsen once every few weeks. These are week day trips but your Squadron offices are aware they happen and soldiers are encouraged to go as an historical educational experience. Please consider it; it is well worth it and an eye opener. In many ways the regime we are opposed to now is not dissimilar that of the Nazi's.

You are free to go.

The British Commanders'-in-Chief Mission to the Soviet Forces in Germany (BRIXMIS) was a military liaison mission which operated behind the Iron Curtain in East Germany during the Cold War.

BRIXMIS existed from 1946 – shortly after the end of the Second World War – until the eve of the reunification of Germany in 1990. Created by an agreement to exchange military missions, the stated object of BRIXMIS – and the Soviet equivalent in the British Zone, SOXMIS – was "to maintain Liaison between the Staff of the two Commanders-in-Chief and their Military Governments in the Zones".

This liaison was undertaken by 31 members – 11 officers and no more than 20 others – appointed to each mission. These liaison staff were issued passes allowing freedom of travel and circulation, with the exception of certain restricted areas, within each other's zone. Such "tours", as they became known, were conducted in uniform and in clearly identifiable vehicles. Nevertheless, although never openly stated, this liaison role also presented an ideal opportunity for the gathering of military intelligence through reconnaissance and surveillance and the occasional 'borrowing' of military matériel. This opportunity was fully exploited by both sides.

BRIXMIS was ideally placed to "test the temperature" of Soviet intentions from its privileged position behind the Iron Curtain. However, and perhaps more importantly, it offered a channel for communication between West and East via its secondary but significant role of liaison – the initial reason for its establishment.

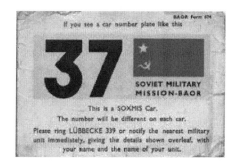

It was still half an hour to lunch and rather than go back to the Squadron or MT the three of us went to the end door of the block - the WRVS and got ourselves a tea and bun.

I have below a short story from our MT Troop Corporal who after recently being promoted to Sergeant was duty Sergeant in charge of the guard. The guard that particular night was provided by 16 Squadron and made up in the main from guys in MT Troop; one of these lads was Titch Kennyford...

I had not long been a Sergeant when I was tasked as Regimental Orderly Sergeant (ROS). On one visit to the guardroom during the late evening I found the Regimental Orderly Officer (ROO) giving instructions to the guard. There had been a Soxmis VW Beetle spotted around the ammunition depot. The instructions were that if the car were to either be seen at the main gate or attempt to try to enter the barracks it was either to be reported in the first instance to Garrison and to be physically stopped. To this end the ROO had some bricks placed at the barrier for the sentry to throw through the windscreen if the car did not stop. I considered this to be completely unrealistic; I asked who was on the gate. The reply was Titch Kennyford, so I immediately left the guardroom to re-brief Titch on his duties. Titch was infamous for obeying instructions to the letter, if you said fuck off to Titch you would very soon be asking where Titch was. I remember arriving in a harbour area one night to see one of the trucks reversing towards two trees and asked Terry Scott where it was going and he said he had told Kennyford to park between them and cam up. Even from 50 yards in the dark it was obvious that you couldn't get a RL in the gap. I started to run but it was too late, it took about half an hour to extricate the truck by felling one of the trees.

I was also too late reaching Titch at the gate, as soon as I ran out of the guardroom and heard several crashes and bangs and there was a VW Beetle, broken windscreen and mounted half way up the far barrier support. Titch said he had held up his hand to stop the vehicle and it wouldn't stop so he threw the brick.

There were obvious questions to ask like why was the barrier up and not down? How come Titch just happen to have the brick ready in his hand?

After the hubbub had died down I very quietly asked Titch the question that he thought he had gotten away with. "Drofynnek didn't that used to be your car"? "Yes, I sold it to a guy in 43 Sqn and he is now refusing to pay me the full amount". Titch was known as Drofynnek thanks to the Sloth's (Bob Groves) habit of speaking English backwards, hence Kennyford became. Drofynnek.

I have no doubt that this is a completely genuine story because in BAOR the strangest and most far-fetched things happened regularly.

On Thursday Taff, Toj and I picked up the course paperwork from Ron Moody. We were flying back to Gutersloh on the Monday following the course ending on the Friday; so like it or not all three of us had the weekend after the course finished, to do what we wanted in the UK, I'm sure that suited me far better than Toj and Taff, both who had family or girlfriend interests in Osnabruck; whereas on the Friday following the course I was only too happy to head west and visit gran and mates in Winsley.

On the Friday, with snow again falling, Tojo and I caught the bus to Gutersloh, Taff was delivered directly from home by Utta.

We split up following the connecting bus journey between Luton and Kings Cross; I was doing the reverse of the same journey I'd done just over three months earlier.

Back to Liverpool Street via the Circle Line, I took the through train to Great Yarmouth. A telephone call home and dad picked me up; twenty minutes later and I was home with my family.

I brought my mum and dad 200 cigarettes to share, the maximum allowed in 1974 through customs and for my dad a bottle of Myres black rum, costing next to nothing from the NAAFI, this was for his birthday the following day.

It was good to be home, but also in a way odd... I didn't live here; this wasn't my house, in fact it felt less like home now than it had during my time in Dover. I'd grown up, I'd become independent and I lived in a barrack room with other guys doing more or less as I wished. I felt that my parents still viewed me as their child and son and that I was back under house rules again. Anyway it was only for thirty six hours and I'd be off again – go with the flow Stevie.

That evening was spent bringing my parents and bro up to date with what I'd been doing the last few months. I wrapped dad's bottle and very late went to bed.

Mum and dad both had to work in the morning so Pete and I kicked our heels around the house. In the afternoon we went to Yarmouth and in the evening went for a fish and chip sit-down supper in 'The Globe' at Blofield; dads choice of birthday meal.

I left around 1100 the following morning, I told mum a white lie that I was flying straight back to Germany the following Friday. I thought she'd be upset if I said I was off to spend the weekend in

Wiltshire; I'd done this numerous times while at Dover and it hadn't gone down well.

By the time I got to Liphook I was feeling groggy, I wondered if I was coming down with something. I called the duty driver who came over from Bordon and picked me up.

Bordon was another old style camp; built initially in the late eighteen hundreds, knocked down rebuilt and added to; it consisted of both Spider and brick buildings rabbling over quite a large area.

We were housed in the brick barracks on the west side of the main road, they looked out over a square and garages and workshops on the far side. These we would discover housed the 'Pigs' and also the classrooms where training took place. I'm digging deep into the memory banks now, the rooms held roughly six beds and on the course with us was another six or seven guys. There weren't many of us. Taff and Toj turned up then we found the cookhouse and had a meal.

Monday morning I woke up feeling awful but struggled through the morning classroom theory looking forward to being out of a stuffy classroom after lunch. In the afternoon we were split into two groups and shown the vehicle; we were talked through all the working parts, the engine and the drivers cab. We were allowed to clamber over the thing and become familiar with it. We were warned how it was top heavy and putting two wheels on a curb that was not necessarily that high could flip the thing over. The brakes were crap; designed initially to stop a one ton light vehicle not a five ton (unladen) armoured upgrade. You had to stand on the pedal to bring it to a stop.

That was it for Monday. I went back to the room and went to bed, I felt ghastly and had a terrible cough.

I struggled through another theory session the first couple of hours of Tuesday morning and the practical driving around the barracks in the afternoon. The weather was really shitty and with a March wind howling through the open drivers hatch doing my cough no favours at all.

Wednesday we were educated on how the 'Pig' is used on the streets in Northern Ireland how we needed to drive it - the pitfalls and idiosyncrasies. We were shown training films on an 8mm projector of the 'Pig' in use on the streets of the province and a demonstration on how easily the thing could tip over. I'd seen news footage of the troubles on the TV but these 8mm training films were taken by the MOD and they showed a different side to the troubles they really were the real deal. After tea break we took two 'Pigs' out for a run around the local area taking it in turns to drive. In the afternoon I stayed in the barrack room I felt like death.

Thursday I gave up; I reported sick in the morning a spent the day dosed up with cough linctus and paracetamol in bed.

That evening Taff and Toj came back and asked how I felt, I was lying on my pit reading my notes, I still felt groggy but knew the following day I would need to sit the theory test which was held in the afternoon, in the morning there was a practical driving assessment. I only hoped I could get myself up and about...

Taff waited till we were alone...

'Hey mate, look what I got,' he said waving a couple of sheets of paper under my nose.

'What've you got there,' I asked him.

'The question papers mate; they were sitting there in the filing cabinet behind the instructor's desk. No one around so I had a peek and hey-presto... you can't look a gift horse in the mouth can you. Not my fault is it? The bloody cupboard should've been locked. Look, what we'll do is run through these and get the answers off Pat; that's the theory taken care of. In the morning I'll ask Jonesy (The Sergeant instructor) if he's willing to sign you off on the practical, after all you had no problem driving the fucking thing so it shouldn't be a problem. You've been ill but you'll still walk away with a pass. What's not to like?'

I just lay there grinning.

'If he insists you do the practical - well, you'll just have to drag yourself out there.'

'Let's see how I feel in the morning Taff, I may be ok to drive. All the same the question papers are bloody handy, are you going to look at it?'

'Course I am, what do think? That I'm going to sit there tomorrow and struggle when I've given the bloody questions to you? Not likely, we'll get some scoff and go through them. Are you in Toj?' Taff directed his question to Tojo sitting on his bed.

Tojo looked a bit reluctant… he was an honest type of guy, also a Corporal.

'I suppose so, look a bit odd if you two passed and I failed; though you better know I don't support this and if you're found out Taff I know fuck-all about it.'

Toj was a lance-jack and he had responsibilities…

'We won't get found out, Christ I've got em now, I'm not likely to try and smuggle em back in am I; we'll memorize the answers and burn the papers out the back.' He said jokingly.

'Yeah, well, what if they've counted them? What if there was only one set of papers for each of us and tomorrow they come up one short; what then?'

'Nothing mate, that's what. Do think they'll say put yur hand up if you nicked a question paper? Yeah, right, they won't say fuck all they'll just think they miscounted and print another… they may think we nicked one but they won't say fuck-all.'

I stayed in the room; my two mates said they'd bring me back some tucker.

That evening we scrutinised the question papers and looked up the answers from our note books, we had to get one or two wrong it would look mighty odd if the three delegates from Sixteen all got one hundred percent, especially me who'd missed half the course.

Friday I'd picked up a bit, I was still coughing but felt better. It was raining stair-rods outside.

'Stay in mate, you'll make yourself worse being out in that shit, we'll try and get you off the practical, then all you do is sit in a warm classroom this afternoon. Finish – pass – Liphook, London and home.'

They brought me back a bacon butty and a brew and I waited to hear the outcome. Ten minutes later Toj stuck his head round the door. 'Stay in here Stevie, you're being signed-off the practical; in fact we may all be if the weather doesn't clear up. The instructors don't fancy going out in this, we'll get soaked with the hatches open and we can see fuck-all with them closed.

Keep you posted.'

At tea break it still hadn't let up and it was decided that the theory would take place, we'd all be signed-off on the practical and we could be out the place directly after lunch.

I joined the others in the classroom at 1030 and the papers were dished out. The three delegates from Sixteen kept a straight face; sure enough the paper was the one Taff had turned up with the previous evening. The papers were collected. We three passed with marks in the nineties. A quick debrief and it was lunch. The truck would take those requiring transport (some UK based bods

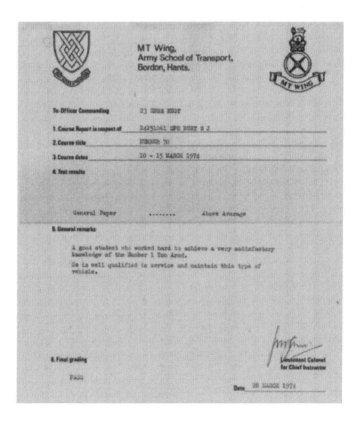

140

had brought their own cars), to the station at 1330. We parted at Waterloo; I'd meet Taff and Toj at Luton on Monday.

I'd last seen my gran as I limped my broken Midget away from King Alfred Way six months earlier. She was well and so was her vicious Jack Russel Trixie. I had a great weekend with my mates going into Bath Saturday afternoon, around the pubs of Bradford-on-Avon Saturday night. Sunday afternoon I caught the bus to Trowbridge to see Clare who came over from Melksham, it was a slow afternoon we couldn't do much it was raining and the cinema by this time had closed. We drank coffee; I told her stories of what I'd been up to... well the clean ones anyway. She was working in the International stores in Melksham. We walked back to the bus station, kissed and promised to keep in touch. That night we had a few beers in the Stars and Monday found me once again heading to London on the intercity 125.

The date was 19th March 1974 what would come next.

Search team training

Work had finished by the time we got dropped off the bus outside the education centre. I read orders and noted I wasn't mentioned for any duties the following day. That was a relief; I'd come back up to the room following parade and sort myself and my kit out.

Eric Brown had returned from Cyprus and there was another addition to our room, there were now four of us with a new lad from Rochdale - Ginge Ruddock.

I was unpacking when Cozy and Ray came in.

'Yur back then? How was it?'

'Yeah, it was good mate – interesting. I was a bit crook during the week and missed a day but passed anyway, they're a bitch of a thing to drive though.'

'We got news for you mate.' They were both grinning.

'What's that then?' I asked warily.

'Yur gunna be a section driver in Ireland, not only a section driver but our section driver and wait for it... we - that is section 11Bravo will be going to Chatham to do a Search Course at the Bomb Disposal School. We, along with a section from two and three Troops are going to be a specially trained Engineer search team eh? What d'ya think of that, bonnie lad.' This was Ray talking.

'Bloody hell, nothing like being asked.' I said. 'When's all this coming about? Who's in the section? Fur Christ sake start at the beginning.'

'Right, ok, so there's us two and you; two new guys, Ginge Ruddock who's shacked up in this room with you; another new bloke called Wings Horne, ex parachute regiment reenlisted in the Sappers; he's a Pad. Benny Bennett, Cobby and Merv's section boss.'

'And - and,' piped in Cosy. 'We're off to Chatham to do a two week Search Course in ten days' time. What d'ya think of that mate?'

'I suppose I'm going to get told this officially at some point?'

'I guess so, come on lets go up the bar, I'll buy you a beer.' Offered Cozy.

Of course I was still under age... I could go on a course that taught me how to search out booby-traps and devices that could tear me limb from sodding limb, but I couldn't buy myself a beer; how fucking ironic is that.

We left the room and headed for the bar.

The following morning saw me once again standing in front of Timmy Wray and Fred...

'So you passed Burt? Good stuff. How was it?'

I explained the week, leaving out the part where Taff obtained the question paper.

'Good, excellent, well done.

Now some further information for you. As per the OCs announcement in January, it has been decided that the forces operating in Northern Ireland need specially trained search teams; Engineer troops have been carrying out search operations for far too long without the background training in booby traps or any recognised procedures or equipment. This is to change with initially two sections from Three-Three Squadron in Antrim being trained and also three sections from Sixteen, one from each troop. You will be section driver for 11Bravo, Corporal Milton's section. You'll be heading off in ten days' time for two weeks at the bomb disposal school in Chattenden. This is an interesting opportunity Burt. You will gain exceptional knowledge on how the IRA conduct their IED warfare, the tricks they use and the way the devises are put together. You'll be trained how to find them and how to deal with them; possibly even neutralise them. Both Corporal Milton and Corporal Cobb requested you as the section driver and I trust you don't have a problem with that Burt?'

So there you go, so much for volunteering, 'I trust you don't have a problem with that'... in short you've volunteered like it or not.

'Oh, and there will be an extra payment for this duty... a form of danger-money if you like.' Your section will continue working in an Engineer role but if a suspect devise or situation is phoned in, you'll have the kit with you. Then one or more of our search sections will be called-up to deal with it. You'll expose the device for the ATO (Ammunitions Technician Officer) who'll take it from there. Staff Dobson will be in charge of the three search sections; no doubt he'll be talking to all of you prior to you leaving for Chattenden. Any questions? No – good; now I suggest you find Corporal Milton; your duties with 11Bravo start from now, dismissed.'

It was all well and good telling me I was now a part of 11Bravo but I was still a part of the MT and the driver of the G1098 wagon. This I brought up with Merv. He would talk to Fred Ludlow who in turn would talk to Staff Scott.

This was quickly sorted; I stripped all the tools from the truck and handed them in to Paddy at the same time drawing the kit for a long wheel-base Land Rover and signing for both vehicle and a three quarter ton GP (general purpose) trailer. With the Land Rover came the responsibility of the Signals communication equipment a C13, a C42 or both.

It had been some time since I'd used either the C13 HF or the C42 VHF vehicle mounted radio sets; I was rusty and in need of some refresher training, this I mentioned to Scotty who told me to go down to the sigs store and get Gerry or Geoff to run through the tuning procedures with me and anything else I needed to brush up on.

The other big change that had taken place in the week we'd been at Bordon was that both Regiments seemed to have come alive. The weather had changed; garage doors were open vehicles were brought out and run up on the hard standing. The barrack was buzzing, I hadn't realized in the time I'd been at Roberts just how many vehicles there were on the site and different types – Land Rovers, Stalwarts, APCs, Ferret Scout cars, Trucks of all different types, four ton, ten ton and the huge REME recovery Scammell's (Pioneers) with rear mounted cranes; the 'Wreaker' as they were called was a serious go anywhere do anything bit of kit, although a relic of the second world war, that would, as we entered the second half of the seventies decade be replaced with the Scammell Crusader a far easier to drive and handle wagon, but not a patch on the beast it replaced. 43 Squadron had their own assortment of tracks and trucks loaded with support equipment as well as 31 Armoured Squadron with their bridge layers and other stuff; hundreds of vehicles everywhere you looked.

Me and Cozy taking a break while training at Sennelager

When I returned to Roberts Barracks in 2007 there was only a single Engineer Squadron based there; they occupied the old REME singlies block by the back gate. The rest of the buildings, those that weren't closed up and unused, of which there were many, were occupied by the RA – The Gunners. What struck me so hard that day in 2007 was the lack of vehicles; there were next to no military vehicles on the camp at all. All those rows of garages, full during the cold war era were empty. Not even a Land Rover to be seen. I asked the young Sergeant who showed us round, the reason for this and he told me that all vehicles were deployed in theatre; meaning where they needed to be i.e - Iraq, Afghanistan or other; no longer in Germany. Any operations or training had all but ceased in Germany. The guys used their own cars when they needed to and claimed petrol expenses where appropriate. A strange set up.

So this was it – count down to operation Banner. From now on most of our days would be spent at Tin City, Sennelager practicing patrolling, dealing with crowd and riot control, property entry, vehicle and personnel check points, simulated ambush procedures.

It was hard work, it was as realistic as the crowds and supervising NCO's could make it, it was nerve racking and at times even though only training with the use of (supposedly friendly) adversaries, it was dangerous – after all a flying brick is a flying brick regardless of who chucks it; if it hits you it hurts or more...

We in 11B were lucky; we had four guys who'd done previous Banner tours. Merv, Cobby and Benny the Belfast tour in 1972 when Sixteen had gone out with the Regiment in an infantry role and Wings who'd done a tour with one of the Para Regiments; for us new-boys their experience and stories were a great help.

On March 29th twenty five of us - one Staff Sergeant, three Corporals, three Lance Corporals *(including Lance Corporal Paddy MacM who was now part of three troop and been picked as 3Tp search team 2i/c)* and the rest Sappers left for the UK.

A truck took us and our baggage to Gutersloh where we joined the throng of squaddies and Pads-wives and kids on the Britannia flight to Luton. It was a late afternoon Friday flight, no trip home prior to the course this time, we spent the night in a dormitory at the Union Jack club behind Waterloo Station.

The recollections below are from Benny...

When we arrived in the UK for the course we stayed in the Union Jack Club the first night as we were too late to get the train to Chatham; we went to a Disco behind Ronnie Scots jazz club in Firth Street because it was the only place we could get a drink. We were the only white guys in a place full of black guys? It was one pint and go, really intimidating...

We arrived in Brompton Barracks, the Royal Engineers ancestral home after lunch Saturday.

We were housed in one of the lovely old buildings that surround the Brompton Barrack parade square. Over the weekend we settled in visiting the town and drinking holes which were quite familiar, most of us having previously carried out training courses in either Chatham or Chattenden. Mick briefed us on what would happen. On the Monday morning we would be trucked over to Chattenden where a classroom introduction would take place. Following break - we – the drivers would sign for a long wheel-base Land Rover and trailer. We would then talk through a selection of search kit and equipment (most of it home made and pretty

146

'Heath-Robinson') which from past experience had been found useful or even invaluable in the course of search operations in the province. From that point on and for the next nine days we'd learn all the bomb disposal school could teach us about IEDs - types, placement, initiators, how to search for them on the ground, how to spot them from the air; the solid and liquid composition used in their manufacture including fertilizers and weed killers containing percentages of nitrogen. We would learn how to search a person, a vehicle with and without a driver present, houses or other buildings both occupied and unoccupied; roadways, farms and farmland. They would also pass-on to us many recorded scenarios and incidents that had happened to previous teams on the ground in both rural and urban environments and the thought and planning that the Provo's put into, not only the live devices, but also the hoaxes that would draw us into their killing zone. From these live scenario's we would learn the right and wrong way to tackle a situation, when to move forward, when to wait and watch. It was going to be a very intense nine days.

It had been a boozy weekend and we were all woolly headed when we climbed aboard the wagon for Chattenden on the Monday morning; there were heaps of pubs in Chatham and Gillingham, many were pubs frequented by Engineers, others by Matelot's from the Navel dock yard, pubs that both groups considered their own; but there were the odd one or two that both soldiers and sailors would frequent and drink side by side. Brawls would break out quite regularly in these pubs. One such pub was the Army and Navy Hotel on the Junction of Dock Road and The Brook, this was a very popular place, a stone's throw from Brompton, Kitchener and the Naval dock yard.

The difference between the two services was very obvious – the Sailors of both sexes had to walk out in uniform. (I suppose I should use the word 'gender' in our now politically correct world, but as this book is far from politically correct from the start, I'll just give political correctness a miss).

147

So there we'd stand; Sappers in civi's and Sailors in uniform supping our pints.

The poker that stoked the fire of course was the WRNS (Wrens) the Women's Royal Naval Service.

The attraction here and I don't wish to sound like Rodney from 'Only Fools and Horses,' was the uniform... A group of squaddies with a few beers inside them with a bunch of lassies in uniform looking more delectable by the pint was a recipe for a punch-up; no not with the women, but with the Matelots who thought the Wrens their own private property.

When things got heated... watch out, because it was the Navy's Military Police unit from the dock yard that would invariably turn up to sort things out and they were a right bunch of thick-headed bastards who wouldn't think twice of laying in with the baton. You'd wake up or come round in the dockyard cell block which would seriously spoil your day.

I did get off with a lovely Wren trainee, Annabelle who made my last week of the course most enjoyable.

The Wrens had to be back inside the dock yard by 2200, or booked in by that time and not a second later. The rules were really strict and we'd head back from town in plenty of time; if she was late back then her shore privileges (as Navy called them. Chatham Naval Dockyard was in fact called HMS Pembroke and Naval terminology applied.) would be banned for x-number of days. As I previously mentioned the girls had to walk out in uniform, this included very solid, yet practical, frumpy low heeled shoes which done nothing to enhance the girl's legs or overall sexy appearance... that's unless of course, you've a thing about frumpy shoes? I didn't. To get round this they would put a pair of 'heels' in their bags and change shoes when out of view of the main gate, or with arrival at said venue; much better.

The thing was they had to change back again prior to signing in. I have fond memories of standing on Dock Road snogging goodnight to Anna as the minutes ticked by; with seconds to spare she'd dive into her bag change into her sturdy shoes and go flying down the road with skirt billowing and her little hat ribbon fluttering behind her, being held on the head with one hand... Ahhh, memories are made of this eh?

Now - I went back to Chatham in 2016, the first time in... let's see now... forty years. I visited the dockyard museum and while there took a nostalgic look at the road where for a week in 1974 I'd watched the flying Anna. Something wasn't right. I remember standing at the top of a slight slope with the road running between two high walls and a gate at the bottom. The gates still there but the layout has changed. I'm guessing the high wall bordering Dock road has been taken down. Still as I say it was yonks ago and I may have some memory distortion.

Still Anna was a week away and we were now climbing out of a truck outside the Bomb Disposal School in Chattenden. (Now *called EOD, Explosive Ordnance Disposal*). Parked in front of us were three long wheel-base Land Rovers with three quarter ton trailers attached. These we would be signing for later in the day, for our use during the course.

(At this point reader I am going to go into some depth regarding our first couple of days at Chattenden and the syllabus contained within our course. The subject matter was complex, not only the ingenuity of the devices and planning ranged against us but also our counter measures. The date was 1974, The IED war (compared with today) was largely in its infancy but gaining in complexity on an almost monthly basis. We were to a great extent pioneers for the present day sophisticated search teams that are operating in Iraq, Afghanistan and other areas of conflict. What is now referred to as 'EOD' was still referred to by the post war name of Bomb Disposal and the modern term of 'IED' was still the Booby Trap. Our equipment as you will read was rudimentary in extreme in comparison to what is being used in the present day.

On our arrival in Ballykelly we had a list of items we wanted to buy and concept drawings of stuff to have made by our brilliant workshop.

A bomb disposal Sapper today, if taken back to the early seventies would probably look at our equipment and wonder how we lived. The wheelbarrow, a remotely controlled robot designed in 1972 for the bomb disposal teams (now an incredibly versatile and indispensable piece of kit) was a new kid on the block, still largely untested and its operating parts limited to carrying a camera and using a very basic remote control arm, not dissimilar to a kiddies remote control toy. I seem to remember being told there was only one in operation in the whole Province, the second one being constantly under repair. Where the wheelbarrow goes today, the search team Sapper went in 1974.

The soldiers search and bomb disposal PPE of today, lightweight and amazing strong polycarbonate and Kevlar wasn't even dreamt off. Ours was a motor cycle crash helmet with off-the-shelf visor and so called body armour, a steel plate an inch thick encased in canvas. However we did live, we carried out these search duties and survived – because we were well trained and professional; oh, and also a bloody sight sharper than our opposition).

We entered the classroom where three Royal Engineer bomb disposal instructors waited for us; a Sergeant and two Corporals.

'Please take a seat gentleman,' the Sergeant said. We sat.

When we were eventually all seated the Sergeant began...

'Good morning men.'

'Good morning,' we mumbled. None of us sounded that sharp including Mick.

The Sergeant said nothing; all three of them just looked at us and then at each other.

'Pass round the photos Corporal and we'll start again.'

'Right Sarg.'

The two corporals picked up four stacks of photos from a table.

'Right men, we'll distribute these among you, please study them and pass them between yourself, we will return in ten minutes.'

They left the room...

Boy did we have a shock.

The photos they had left us with were actual IED incident photos; photos where people - both civilian and soldiers, had either been caught in an unsuspecting blast such as a dustbin bomb, a waste bin bomb, or a culvert bomb, or had pulled, stood on, or opened the wrong thing at the wrong time. They were all labelled with date time and in some cases names. They were without doubt very graphic and very gruesome. They showed injuries in horrendous detail, some photos where body parts were so badly destroyed you wondered how many people were involved or what bit went where. In among the flesh and bone were the other aspects of daily lives – bags, prams, suitcase, duffle bag or shoe; some with a foot still in it. Civilian vehicles and military vehicles, on their roofs or sides, burning or in bits.

The intension was to shock us from the first moment – to wake us up and to let us know the role we had volunteered for was no game, it was without doubt, deadly serious.

They – our instructors had watched us amble into the classroom laughing and joking, half hung over and still half asleep. These photos were our first morning wake up call. I've never forgotten them in forty years.

Mick said in no uncertain terms – Right you lot, they're giving us a message, sharpen up and lets look like we mean business when they come back in.'

After ten minutes the instructors returned. We were all sitting up looking sharp and attentive.

'So, let's start again. 'Good morning men.'

'Good morning Sarg,' we replied, with far more vigour.

'That's better... (pause)

Men this course is no joke. You've viewed the photographs we left you with; I hope those photos were your wake-up call. They are the reality in this job if you should fuck-up; gruesome eh? All taken from actual situations on the ground, and believe it or not, all were taken over a very short period of time. Carnage like this is a daily occurrence in Ulster. If you do not wish to undertake this training in a serious manner and give the subject the respect it deserves say so now. I will arrange for you to be RTUed...

I do not want anyone on this course who is not prepared to give one hundred percent, I do not want anyone on this course because they've been told they've got to do it, I don't care what your Squadron has to say about it, I will return you to your unit, today if needs be. I do not want anyone on this course because they fancy a couple of weeks in Blighty.'

He was surveying us all as he spoke.

If... during this course, or at the end, I do not consider a person capable, or of the disposition - and by that I mean having the right mental attitude to carry out the duties required of a search team operative, you will not be carrying out those duties on the ground in Ulster. Is that understood?

'Yes Sarg.' We all said.

'Good, now let's get down to business. First, sticky label in front of you please write your name on it and wear it on your chest for the next couple of days, until we get to know you, we will address you by your Christian name.

'My name is Sergeant A, this is Corporal B, and the third member of our training team here is Corporal C. We will be joined from time to time by Captain D RE who is an Ammunitions Technician's Officer. He will be giving an insight into their role in the Province and how they interact with you.

The concept of the specialist search team is a new one and it makes sense that we Engineers provide the sections to carry it out; initially anyway. Over the course of time it may prove worthwhile training teams from other units... still that's' some way off.

Improvised explosive devices are becoming the weapon of choice for the Provo's they are learning the art of explosive ordnance and learning it very quickly – we need to keep up with them and have teams that are trained to deal with the rapidly growing problem. From now until tea break I'll give you a run down on what we're up against in the way of devises; after tea we'll look through the kit in the trailers and one from each section can sign the chit. They'll be in your charge until the course finishes on the seventeenth. You will be here in the UK over Easter, for those wishing to visit family in the UK you are free to do so. However we do have a final classroom day on the sixteenth, gear returned on the morning of the seventeenth, I believe you have the evening flight back to Gutersloh from Luton. So let's begin gents:

Gentlemen the composition and initiation of IEDs, or as you've been used to calling them 'booby traps' are wide ranging. Initiators are as simple as a battery, a clothes peg, a couple of drawing pins and a detonator pushed into a lump of plastic (*PPE, plastic explosive*). From there we work up the sophistication ladder till we arrive at devices activated by radio control. I'm hoping as Sappers you are all trained at least to B3 level in demolitions. You'll be aware that - in the majority of cases, an explosive device needs electricity to initiate the charge? We, when laying and initiating a charge use an EDC; we wind a handle creating a build-up of electricity push a button to send the voltage down the wire to the charge. The Provo's use a battery - either wet cell or dry cell, it matters not.

The simplest device can be made by pressing two drawing pins into the open jaws of a clothes peg, attaching a wire to each pin, one's crimped to the wire from the det, the other leads to the battery terminal, from the other terminal another wire goes again to the other side of the det. The circuit is then live but for the small piece of wood, a wedge, holding the jaws of the peg open, thereby preventing the pins from touching and completing the circuit. What happens when the wedge is removed from the peg?'

He was pointing at Steve A.

'The pins touch and that action completes the circuit Sarg,' replied Steve.

'Correct – that simple little device can be used almost anywhere in any application, the only down side to the charge is you have to hide or anchor the battery. A pull switch - it is almost fool proof. Another take on this is a metal tube with a metal ball bearing inside, a cork in the end with a nail through the cork. You attach it to a door handle. Door handle is pushed down from the outside, switch is on the inside, ball rolls down the tube and connects the nail with the inside of the tube thus completing a metallic circuit; Boom, up she goes taking you with it; known as a trembler or tumbler device. This same little lovely can be used in the ground as a pressure switch; stand on the nail – it presses down onto the base of the tube and again bye bye mummy... need I say more? All three very simple but effective when assembled with care. These are just a few garden shed homemade devices. We then have military switches mechanical and chemical which are obtained by the IRA through Libya and other countries that support terrorism, sadly a great deal of hardware comes also from the USA where there is a great deal of support for the IRA within the Irish communities. The next level of sophistication – light, movement, and noise sensitive switches, hidden in cupboards so when the unsuspecting person opens the door... bang, dead. Where do you find light sensitive switches? Anyone?'

We all sat there looking gormless...

'Come on lads, its simple; how about street lighting, security light activators, these items are all around us. Noise activators are in dictaphones, baby alarms and numerous other everyday devices.

Timing devices... again radio alarm clocks, electronic door locking mechanisms, light timers; innocent everyday items that we never give a thought to. They will all be used against you. Then to top it off we're seeing the new kid on the block the radio frequency controlled device. No wires running to this baby; set off from half a mile away with no tell-tell signs like hundreds of yards of remote wiring.

So that touches on the initiators; now to explosive... You will deal with military grade explosive - C4 - American light brown in colour smells of motor oil, not that common with the Provo's; SEMTEX from the Eastern Bloc was developed and manufactured in Czechoslovakia, originally under the name B1, It is used in commercial blasting, demolition, and in certain military applications it's a reddy orange in colour, one of the worrying aspects of this material it has hardly any distinctive aroma. We suspect that the majority of this stuff is coming in via the Libyans who are making a name for themselves suppling terror groups all over Europe. Other commercial grade explosive, stolen from quarries known as ANFO or AN dash FO, stands for ammonium nitrate fuel oil, it's a widely used bulk industrial explosive. Homemade explosive can be made, as you're probably aware, from chemicals as simple as sugar and weed killer; you may have even made a charge as a kid at school? I know I did. So, fertilizers bearing over twenty eight percent nitrogen we also refer to loosely as ANFO. Ammonium nitrate fertilizers with twenty eight percent or more nitrogen are banned in the Province. If you carry out a rural search and I assure you all, you will, and you come across bags showing a content of twenty eight percent or over whether full or empty you'll nick the farmer concerned. He shouldn't have the stuff. Mixed with diesel in the right proportions it is a potent weapon. They are without doubt gentlemen out to get us any way they can and we've got to be one jump ahead. So that's our taster to the course gents; I hope I've held your interest. Let's go for break, you know where the NAAFI is, back here in fifteen minutes.'

Following break we returned to the classroom and waited to discover what exactly we had in the trailers coupled to our Section long-wheelbase Land Rovers. Tea break had been pretty animated; we'd all been together in the NAAFI except for Mick who'd gone over to the Sergeants mess and the conversation had revolved around the horrendous photos we'd been shown and the simplicity of the devices that caused the carnage. Frightening stuff, we all agreed.

We made sure we were back at the classroom on the dot of half ten. We'd rubbed our instructors up the wrong way once that morning and didn't want to do it again; they weren't the type to cut us any slack for a second offence... well at least on day one.

'Right lads, outside, around the trailers in your sections.'

Each instructor took one of our sections. Sticking out either end of the trailer tilt (cover) were the legs of a step ladder and a three section sliding ladder.

'Ok let's have the covers off'.

A couple of us unhooked the trailer tilt and put it to one side. We peered into the trailer there seemed to be very little in there.

One by one we went through the contents. There were... mine prodders, these we had seen and used many times in training and on exercise, used to slide at an angle into the ground while clearing a safe lane through a mine field. Also there was the standard 4C mine detector, again a commonly used item in Combat Engineering. There was a coil of electric wire on a spool with a plug that fitted the 24 volt dc socket on the Land Rover dashboard; a powerful search type light which looked not dissimilar to the type of security light common on most houses today only bigger and painted green. Three coils of rope, a selection of hooks and carabiners, crow bars, sledge hammer pick axe and six full sand bags and that was pretty much it; in short a bit of an anti-climax. Nothing overly technical at all.

'Right lads, gather round and listen in. I can see you're not impressed with the items in the trailer and you're probably wondering if this is all the kit you'll need. Well the answer is no. Over the next couple of weeks we will use this basic kit. In situations where you think you may need something different or more sophisticated we'll be making notes. It will be very much up to you on the ground in your area of operations to make, buy, or modify tools for the job. The items in these trailers are but the basics. The light, we touched on light sensitive devices. The light and cable would be taken into somewhere like a cellar or attic and left, you would remove yourselves from the area unreeling the cable as you retreated and plug in the light from the dash of the vehicle.

Corporal... who is it? - Merv?' said the Sergeant peering at Merv's name tag.

'That's me - Merv Milton Sarg.' Sang out our section's intrepid leader.

'Right Merv, why would you uncoil the cable back to the socket point rather than unravel it from the vehicle into the building?'

Merv was sharp...

'I'm guessing Sarg, that doing it that way ensures the searcher would be clear of the area before the plug is pushed home.'

'Exactly; well fuckin done Merv. You all follow that? If the cable is unravelled from the safe area it means there is an unprotected plug lying next to a live socket that any prat without thinking can ram home. Not funny if you're in that dark room not knowing if there's a light sensitive device sitting in a corner and wally brain turns the room into a fuckin funfair. If you didn't die in the following blast I'm sure you'd fuckin squash the bastard that done it.

You return to the safe area with the plug; your oppo's with you, you plug in the light knowing that no one – friend anyway, is going to lose their balls. If there is a light sensitive devise in the room it would go up without any harm coming to you guys a safe distance away. However I would advise keeping your head well down as you push the plug in. Any questions?'

The question came from Billy, two troop section corporal.

'What about protection Sarg. Is it just standard piss-pot and flak jacket or do we get something a little more upmarket?'

'Good question Billy and I might add very valid. One of the items not in this trailer but we'll look at after lunch is a set of body armour. We'll show you the body armour that you'll be issued with; it's steel it's thick plate and very heavy, you'll use this for urban searches or in close proximity to a suspected device but not necessarily on a rural search, you could not walk for miles across fields wearing this gear. As for helmets... I'm ashamed to say at present there is nothing substantial to replace the piss-pot. You'll purchase, paint and operate with motor cycle crash helmets and visors, these, if they are not already waiting for you, you'll obtain when you get there. Lads... we are playing catch-up. The Squadron you'll take over from in Ballykelly will have done searches during their tour but will not have had the benefit of visiting our establishment here at Chattenden. They will almost definitely have accumulated equipment as aids to search operations; your task will be to improve on what they've put in place.

Another item we'll look at this afternoon is the baton gun; not rubber bullets but plastic. The simple rubber bullet is being phased out in preference to the plastic round apparently we're killing too many of the bog-dwellers with the rubber bullet. I have my own views on that and I'm sure you have yours. The plastic round will take a door off its hinges. We'll give you a demo of this later in the course. So getting back to the trailer... Rope, three - fifty yard coils, you can carry as much as you like. Used for pulling or moving anything from a distance; open a door, move a cupboard, sofa, table... well just about anything really, tie it to a weight for dropping from height that would set of a trembler activated or pressure switch; get it? Lots of uses. Ladders - the ladders, as obvious as it may sound, are for climbing over things, go over a wall instead of through a gate; form a bridge without touching the ground. Use them for climbing into upper floor windows or through the roof – don't do the expected, do the unexpected and don't hurry; search can be a very slow process... remember, think outside the box lads. Ok let's get the gear back in the trailers and go for lunch; back here at 1330.'

When we returned from lunch and were seated our two Corporal instructors entered the room; one was wearing the armoured vest, with a collar and some kind of ball protector slung between the legs and the other was carrying two different types of baton gun which he laid on the table in front of us.

'Lads this is the body armour you'll be using and wearing during your search operations in Ulster. For those of you on your first tour, this is not a flak-jacket. The flak-jacket; as those who've been before will know, is a relatively lightweight jacket that

158

you wear continually when outside of a safe area. This equipment is somewhat different, not only in weight but also in how to get into it.

In three parts, the main body, the neck, and the scrotum protector. I will now remove it and you'll see how each part effectively overlaps.'

You'll then get the chance to try it out yourselves.'

We watched as our instructor de-velcro'd himself.

'I would hope that in a section of eight you would have a minimum of three sets of this gear, four would be ideal. You Mick, as I/C search troop would have your own set; you could be called forward at any time.'

The main body protector was the first piece to come off, released by ripping free the Velcro fastening on the right side of the body. Your left arm would then pull out of the left arm slot. Beneath the main section there was a further section protecting the pelvic region and a high collar

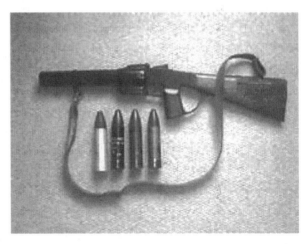

protecting the neck, both containing steel plate and held in place by velcro. I looked at this stuff very sceptically... the legs and arms were completely exposed if you were caught in a major blast it was quite likely you'd spend the rest of your life with no limbs, being fed and having your ass wiped; a frightening prospect. Also it looked incredibly cumbersome, how on earth were we expected to crawl along the ground hunting for devices wearing something that weighed half a hundred-weight and hardly allowed us to turn our heads? The whole get-up looked pretty Heath-Robinson to me.

The armour was put to one side; we were told we could play with them later. The next item or items on the agenda were the two baton guns.

'Right lads, some of you have done one or maybe more than one Op Banner in the past, so you'll be familiar with this piece of hardware,' said our instructor holding up a short weapon with an exceptionally large diameter barrel.

'This is a rubber bullet gun, and this is a spent rubber bullet men, it's on loan from Dave's missus.' He said grinning at one of the Corporals. *(Laughs all round)...* as I said earlier, being phased out in place of the plastic round. There has, over a very short space of time, been numerous fatalities from these rounds, this is most probably due to them not being used correctly, they should not be fired directly at a

person or crowd but bounced off the roadway in front... how that works on grass I don't know, but still that is the way they're supposed to work. Whether or not the softer plastic type will change the statistics we'll need to wait and

see, I very much doubt it. This other weapon has been produced to fire the new supposedly less harmful plastic round; this is it.' He said holding up another large barrelled weapon. The plastic rounds I'm led to believe will be colour coded for density, the black ones being the hardest and the type you'll use for opening door's etcetera. What I'd like you to do for the next twenty minutes is come up and have a look over this equipment, try on the body armour. We have five further sets next door. We'll be using two sets per section when we start on our practical training tomorrow.'

We went forward and in groups tried on the body protection and looked closely at the batons and baton guns. I had to admit I wouldn't want to be hit by one of those rubber bullets... actually I wouldn't want to be hit by the plastic one either.

We went for a break and then settled in for the last part of the afternoon's tuition. This was to do with requirement for our specialist services. Or put simply, search shouts.

Our instructor started again.

'Men, I'm guessing your search team duties will run in parallel with your Engineer tasking. You could be out building a sanger, a VCP or any other Engineer task when the call comes that a suspect device has been reported. It could be a genuine call, it could be a suspect package or a suspicious action that a well-meaning person has phoned in, or it could be a hoax. We'll take these one at a time. They all have one thing in common to your follow up action; well two actually; any takers?'

This was said while looking around at all of us... we were all silent.

'No? Ok, the two things they all have in common is that one, we attend. If we didn't attend and a device went off in a busy street or in the hands of an unsuspecting child the propaganda value to the IRA would be enormous. British army responsible for the death off... get me? All over the fuckin telly. I'll come back to this in a moment. The second thing they all have in common is that you - the search team will not be the first on the scene. You will arrive and set up shop – your safe area - after the infantry cordon is in place. The infantry cordon will protect you from the locals and keep the locals, even if they are hostile which they probably will be, out of harm's way. You – a section of eight men cannot front up with your travelling show, carry out a search and at the same time keep the locals from either being nosey or being plain disruptive, and by disruptive I mean chucking everything under the sun at you. You communicate with your infantry protection and you make sure the cordon is in place before you front up. This lad's is very important indeed.

A body discovered in a country lane... a tout, tortured and bumped off, probably mutilated with a bullet in the back of the head. The last act the Prov's carry out is to place a device under the body or plant a device in the area.

The infantry will seal off the area, but they won't be close... probably stand off a quarter mile, you'll need to decide how close you'll go before stopping and setting up shop.

You'll check the area by chopper from above, you'll look for signs of remote wiring, footsteps in the mud, signs where the wire has been dug into the turf; is the body laying over a culvert? They have to work quickly and not always carefully, this kind of scenario would more often than not be carried out at night, in the dark and rain, as quickly as possible... Why in the rain? Because it never does fuck all else over there but piss down.' (Laughs from us all).

He continued – 'If there is no sign of remote wiring then the next step is the radio sweep. No big bang? Fine, then you've got to start moving in. Look at the body through bino's can you see anything untoward from a distance? The one thing you can't account for is the timer. The Provo's work out how long they think it will take for you to arrive on site, set-up shop and start moving in on the body. The call - the drive - the preparation... they know roughly how long it all takes because they've done it many times before; so they set the timer for... let's say, five hours hoping that you've moved to within a few yards of the target when 'click' the countdown finishes and the device goes off. The only way to counter this is too wait; if need be wait a couple of hours at the scene before you move in. That way, if the timer has been preprogramed it'll go off before you begin operations and before you're close enough to the charge to be damaged. Don't be hassled by the infantry commander who is rushing you because he wants his men out of the area; it's not his blokes who'll go sky high in the blast. So... is the body next to a field? Are there cattle in the field? If so the chances are there is no large device in the field or under the body. Cattle are inquisitive; they'll come to a hedge and watch what's going on, a pressure switch in the field would be set off by the stock; a remote wire could be damaged by a hoof. The Provo's wouldn't want that, it would be a waste of effort and explosive regardless if the cattle belonged to a Prod or a left-footer, no apologies to the Catholic's among you.'

(I had begun to realise that the army made no distinction between its men; their colour, nationality, or religion. The Irish were referred to as Paddies, Mick's or bog-dwellers, Catholics were Fenians or left-footers and Germans were krauts or box-head anyone who wore a turban or head covering was a rag head. If a soldier happened to be one of those then tough, you put up with it or you punched the person's lights out who made the remark. Political correctness was still a long way into the future. MacM was with us. He was in one of the other troop search team sections, second in command, he was Irish and he was Catholic. He just had to lump it. Me I was German, what was referred to as a 'Boxhead' and on a couple of occasions already I'd been called that in fun but the day it was used on me seriously would be the day I had to make up my mind if I was going to nip it).

Do you follow all this lads? If you don't then for fuck sake say so. We'll move on with questions later, the clock is ticking, excuse the pun and we've a great deal to get through.

So going back to the 'every call must be attended' propaganda issue. Our enemy know this. They know if someone rings in, we have to check it out. So if you're called into a known risk area where people live it could well be a hoax – a plan to draw you in and then have a gunman take a pop at you; this is why the cordon is so important, it's highly unlikely that they will plant a device among their own kind, however they will try a shot regardless of the cordon, they know they can shoot – dump the weapon in safe hands where it will be hidden, and get away through the houses and alleyways without getting caught. When the kids disappear indoors and the street is suddenly empty, that's the time to be more vigilant and keep your heads down. The words gone out, the shooters about. Next - how about an area where few people live, an industrial site or a building site with new built, or half built unoccupied houses? This is almost definitely where the device proper will be; and it could be of any type, hidden anywhere, less likely to be a hoax, less likely to find a gunman;

why? The answer to the former - the device when initiated would destroy property and probably only take out foe as in you guys, not friend; the latter - the gunman, unless the shot is taken over a great distance would stand less chance of getting away. So whenever you're called in to any search task analyse the situation, analyse the area; ask the question why? Why is it here? What is the reasoning behind it? How do they plan to get us. From the IRA point of view there is more than one way - as they say, to skin a cat. One final scenario and this is one that is in the extreme and in most cases can't be dealt with by you.

The mass sectarian killing - you saw a couple of photos this morning that show the aftermath of a bomb left in a crowded place and this could be one from either side of the sectarian divide, protestant or catholic walking into a bank, shop, post office, or bar and leaving a timed device; or parking a van or car full of explosive and just walking away. They are not out to get the army, they are out to get their opposition, won't be phoned in and unless someone is very vigilant and quick to clear the area people die. Probably out of your jurisdiction, ATO would be the people called and they would most probably remotely detonate.

Ok lads enough for today, there's three clip-boards up here one per section, decided which of you is going to sign for the vehicle, trailer and gear. Let me have the paperwork back and we'll see you here at 0830 in the morning. Be warned the traffic through Rochester in the mornings is hell; give yourself a good hour to get here. Tomorrow we walk you through an empty house scenario.'

As section I/C Merv signed and we piled into the Land Rover for the trip back to Brompton I drove with Merv alongside me; our six oppo's in the back. It had been a long and intense day. We wound our way out of the barracks down Four Elms Hill on the A228 into Frinsbury the outskirts of Rochester eventually after a slow rush-hour slog we hit the roundabout with the high street and went left over the bridge, another crawl to Military Road left into Dock Road and up the hill past Kitchener and into Brompton; bloody agony.

Our rooms bordered the square, grand buildings indeed dating from the mid-eighteen hundreds; our accommodation was on the far side of the square. Around the corner off the square was the very grand officers mess, *(forty five years later I would be given a guided tour of the officers mess as a member of the Junior Leaders Association, an incredible look at the paintings, memorabilia and silverware the Corp had collected over its history; a rare and real privilege indeed).*

We were accommodated on the second floor and our rooms looked out over the square. Oddly we were allowed to park our vehicles directly in front of the block, actually on the square itself.

The talk on the way back to Chatham had been all about our first day; what we'd been told, what we'd seen and the hardware we had been introduced to; already ideas were being thrown around as to how we could improve our inventory. I got the definite impression that we all realised the seriousness of the role we were training for. However that didn't inhibit our after work activities and no sooner had we returned from the cookhouse it was shower and hit the pubs; after all we were now back in the UK with its antiquated licencing laws. No laying on the pit till ten and then hitting the Winkle like we did back in Traz.

The following morning we fought our way again through the rush hour to Chattenden and were all seated attentively when our instructors entered; in front of us were a number of photocopied handouts and a small book entitled Field Engineering and Mine Warfare, Pamphlet seven, Booby Traps; published nineteen fifty two... nineteen fifty two!? Jesus could this really be the most up to date training pamphlet on the subject? Yes apparently it was... Flicking through I could quickly see the little book was in two parts with a number of chapters covering - general considerations, individual mechanisms, detection & clearance and recording; followed by the usual appendices and figures etc.

There were drawings depicting devices hidden under floor boards in a house, under a tree across a road and one in a toilet cistern; all from another era but still I supposed, quite relevant.

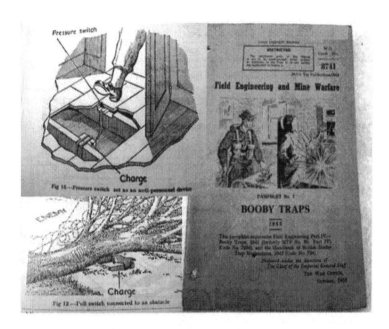

Fig 14.—Pressure switch set as an anti-personnel device

Charge

Charge

Fig 13.—Pull switch connected to an obstacle

Field Engineering and Mine Warfare

BOOBY TRAPS

Now we had our bed time reading material... bye bye Playboy and Mayfair.

Our instructors told us we would be taken to a building which had been prepared with numerous devices to show us what we could expect during our training and also when we were on the ground for real in Northern Ireland. We would be walked through the building, the hidden devices and types pointed out. Each device would be discussed and we would put forward our collective ideas on how we could, with the indispensable help of a sniffer dog, discover them without necessarily initiating them and avoid being harmed by them. This was how we spent the morning.

After lunch our three NCO instructors disappeared, no doubt to set up the practical exercise for the following day.

We had an afternoon with the ATO, the Ammunitions Technicians Officer. This was a very interesting session, he went through his role in the neutralizing of the charge, what Forensics could learn from the way the change was put together; there was a heap of information in a neutralized device. He explained the 'Wheelbarrow' and showed us slides of the remote machine in action. Although in its infancy in 1974 it would go on to become a game changer and a life saver, advancing in technical ability at a rapid rate. He told us of how our work would be helped by the sniffer-dog and later in the course a dog would be brought in to give a demonstration on its explosive finding prowess. He explained how forensic science aided in conviction, how the minutest speck of explosive could be found on skin and clothing or in a car. How rifling in the barrel of a weapon could be linked to a spent round taken from a body. All very interesting stuff.

Wednesday and Thursday were both practical days searching buildings within the barrack area. We were taught what to look for when searching occupied houses, where a weapon may be hidden; a pistol in a potty with baby shit on top of it; up the chimney, false walls or backs to cupboards, water tanks in the loft space. The list was endless...

Thursday after work our section piled onto the Gillingham - Canterbury train for a good piss-up and party; it was to celebrate my birthday, a special one, my eighteenth; at last I was officially old enough to drink and officially old enough to go into the Squadron bar and order a pint. It was a long time coming, I'd started at five years old with a Mackason given to me with my Sunday lunch by dad way back in Saint Nicholas Close, Winsley.

We done all the pubs in the centre of Canterbury and we were all well-oiled for the train journey back to Gillingham. Disembarking in Gillingham we laughed and sang our way along Jeffery Street toward Brompton barracks, all was going swimmingly until Benny and Wings spotted a beautifully laid out front garden containing a giant windmill and garden gnome, both around three foot tall. They had to have them. The theft of these two far from small garden accessories, was not carried out with stealth or in silence; oh no, six of us stood on the pavement laughing fit to bust while Wings and Benny as blatant as you like walked through the gate, picking up said accessories and carried them off... I seem to remember both of them wearing the decoration on their heads. We got to Brompton, the guard on the gate let us through, we were obviously drunken Sappers, who else would try entering a military barrack wearing a gnome and a windmill singing *about the hairs on her dickydidoe hanging down to her knees....* I'm sure as he watched us stagger past he muttered, 'someone will be in the shit tomorrow.'

A couple of steps led from the path surrounding the square up to the door of the accommodation. Both the gnome and the windmill were placed on the top step, one either side of the door; they looked lovely and quite at home had they been in a residential street... perhaps not quite so fitting in a very imposing Victorian barrack.

We drunkenly went to bed, it had been a great night and the evening had proved we were a section that got on well and would work together well over the next six months.

The following morning, Friday, a very hungover section left for breakfast and were reminded of the previous night's antics by the garden ornamentation still standing on the top step.

'You want to get rid of those,' Merv told Wings and Benny. However they had other ideas, they would leave them there for the day and return them to their place in the owners garden in the dead of night. As if the owner hadn't notice they'd gone?

Our three sections weren't the only Sappers occupying the block; in fact all the rooms surrounding the square accommodated guys doing a multitude of courses; all made their way to the cookhouse that morning via the road between our block and the officer's mess. By the end of breakfast the word was well out about the gnome and windmill on the top of our steps.

Mick Dobson, also at breakfast, didn't get to hear about the prank in the Sergeants mess; at this early hour the joke hadn't got that far, but he saw them as soon as he joined us in front of the block for the trip over to Chattenden.

'Get the bloody things out of sight! Jesus Christ where do they come from? Who nicked them? Come on I want to know!?'

Everyone was looking at the two culprits; there was no getting out of it for Benny and Wings.

'If this gets back to RHQ... if you were seen and the owner ends up phoning the Adjutant there'll be hell to pay, honestly, you two bloody morons. Corporal Milton, were you a party to this?' Asked Mick looking daggers at Merv.

'No Staff, I knew nothing about it.' Lied Merv scowling hard at Wings and Benny.

'Right - two section and three section get going to Chattenden. Bennett, Horne, you do remember where these came from don't you?' The lads from two Troop and three Troop sections were grinning as they mounted the Land Rovers for work.

'Think so Staff,' they mumbled in unison.

'Right, no time now, but straight after work, and I mean as soon as we're back here from across the river, those items will be returned to their rightful owners. And Corporal Milton this section is to remain in Chatham this weekend. No going anywhere. Is that understood? That also includes you Corporal Milton.'

'Yes Staff; Benny, Wings, put those things in your room and let's get going.'

Benny and Wings disappeared back to the block and Mick Dobson climbed in next to me, Merv squeezed in the back and minutes later we too were off, five minutes behind our other sections.

I had to feel sorry for Merv; Benny was a class act on his own and now with Wings in the Troop and both in his section he had a lot to contend with, Wings saw himself as a bit of a cool ex-Para who was up for anything and Benny was having none of it. They were almost in competition who could outdo who in the assing-around stakes and Merv had to pick up the pieces.

I pushed it to the limit on the drive over to Chattenden but there was no way I could catch the other two sections in the rush hour traffic. We got down to the big roundabout on the Finsbury road and there we were gridlocked. Some girl in Ford Anglia had crossed the Bill Street Road junction with no exit and all the roads were jammed solid. After being totally stationary for another good five minutes the lads done no more than jump out the back and physically picked the car up with the girl in it and moved it out of our way... on we went.

By the time we got to the classroom our oppo's were seated and waiting; the Sergeant instructor sitting on the edge of the desk recapping the previous days exercise.

'Sit down gents; I see you didn't bring the extra member of your section.' Obviously he'd been given the low-down on why we were late. We quickly sat down and our instruction resumed. However this wasn't the end of it. Mick was called to the phone during the morning break; it was the RSM from Brompton.

We had been spotted taking the gnome and the windmill and it wasn't rocket science to work out that we were Squaddies from either Brompton or Kitchener (The Navy would have been in uniform and not singing raucous army songs). A call to both barracks and questions to the duty guard quickly brought forth the answer; yes a group of eight had entered the barracks at midnight carrying a gnome and a windmill. Yes they had headed off across the Square to the end block; yes they were ratassed and yes most lads going to breakfast had spotted the gnome and windmill on the way. Yes the second floor rooms in the end block were taken by a troop from Sixteen Squadron training in search at Chattenden.

Mick came back from the phone fuming. He'd had a right ear bashing from the RSM. Mick had assured the RSM that the items would be returned; a profound personal apology would be made to the owner by those concerned. Nothing like this would ever happen again and those responsible would be duly dealt with on return to home unit in ten days' time.

The morning began with personal search procedures, how to search a person at a check point; the places on the body where a weapon or a device could be hidden - push-chairs, prams – distractions such as screaming kids, aggressive dogs, stinking nappies... what better place to hide a few 9mm rounds then in your brats nappy after he or she (or it) has dumped a bucket-full. We then went on to vehicle searches where to look, how to look, what to look for. False engine parts that didn't actually belong on the engine but would hoodwink a soldier or police officer just taking a

170

quick glance. Signs that trim had been removed or false trim added... There was no end to the information we had to absorb.

We had a short recap session after lunch before knocking of early for the weekend, however we 11Bravo would not be going far in the next 48 hours.

Walking out of the main gate carrying a windmill and a gnome while half the population of Brompton is heading off for the weekend was not quite so funny as it had been eighteen hours earlier entering with the items drunk in the middle of the night.

Cat-calls and whistles followed 11Bravo as the eight of us walked back toward the house in Gillingham from where we'd stolen the ornamentation. Mick had made sure in no uncertain terms that we would all be involved with the apology. We could be thankful for small mercies; we didn't have to march as a squad or go in uniform.

However the windmill was suffering, the sails had fallen of and it was really not in the same condition it had been when it left the garden eighteen hours earlier. Five of us waited at the gate as Merv, Benny and Wings rang the doorbell. A lady opened the door, Merv explained we were here to return her gnome and windmill; that we were very sorry for the inconvenience caused and it was a case of high spirts due to us all passing our course exams, (lying git) and at the same time celebrating my birthday. Her husband was not yet home from work; but she stood over us as they were repositioned in her garden. On closer inspection she said 'you've broken the windmill; it's damaged beyond repair, you'll have to pay for it.'

Benny coughed up the dosh.

As quickly as we could we evacuated the scene of the crime.

That evening we hit the Army and Navy, the bar downstairs. Once again Benny and Wings were on form, showing-off and trying to out-do each other this time by eating spiders, which they either ate or dropped in the Wrens drinks. The girls were aghast, a couple running to the toilet to be sick, one girl sitting between Wings and Benny didn't bat an eyelid so Benny went outside and picked a bunch of Daffodil's growing on the roundabout which he presented to the Wren has she sat there holding them the lads done no more than snap the heads off and eat them. This girl was a real sport and joined in claiming they tasted like spring onions.

It broke the ice and this is the point I started chatting to the delectable Annabelle, the two of us had been eyeballing each other over the top of our glasses for a while until I plucked up courage to initiate more meaningful (tongue in cheek; my own not hers) conversation. As I mentioned earlier you took your life in your hands chatting up the Wrens if their male counterparts were around. Still this particular evening all was well, the place was quiet. I took an early departure; arm round Anna to wolf-whistles and lurid comments to somewhere a bit less chaotic.

We ended up having a lovely weekend in each other's company, (sounds a bit naff doesn't it? Naff but true).

The following week we returned to our training and covered a wide range of search scenario's, including vehicle, property (occupied and unoccupied) and rural. We were taken out into the countryside, the training areas at Mereworth Woods near Maidstone in Kent and Crowborough East Sussex. For these rural search exercises a small Chopper was provided and a few of us along with our NCOs were given the opportunity to be shown what to look for in the way of give-away signs from the air. We had a most interesting search/sniffer dog demonstration where explosive was hidden in one of the empty training houses and the dog sent in to find it. A spaniel called 'Blaster', what a great name.

We were to find in the coming months just how valuable the dog could be and also the perils of ignoring the signs they convey.

The evenings in the week I shrugged-off my section buddies and met up with Annabella; Thursday was rapidly upon us; but for a day's recapping the coming Tuesday the course was all but over. Most of us with family in the UK hit the station for the train home for an Easter Weekend. I said my goodbyes to Annabella Thursday evening, she was going home to Worthing for the weekend but wouldn't be back in Chatham till Wednesday – an extended Easter break due to her great gran celebrating her hundredth birthday.

We would write to each other... yes of course we would, for all of two months.

I got home to find my car had been sold and I had the grand sum of £200.00 in cash. Considering I had spent £250.00 on my MG, another £100.00 to insure it and over £100.00 on bits to rebuild it following the hospital wall prang I was well out of pocket. I was still paying for it with a very costly high interest bank loan and should've used the proceeds of the sale to clear some of the debt... however; ever foolish where money was concerned I just kept the cash and frittered it away. More than a few times over the coming couple of years would I wish I'd cleared that loan when I had the chance.

It was good to be home for Easter; I quite possibly wouldn't see my parents and brother again until I had my R&R (rest and recuperation) long weekend half way through my Northern Ireland deployment.

Monday I returned to Chatham.

Tuesday - our final day was spent signing in our kit and having a debrief QA with our instructors. 'Remember what I told you lads,' summarised our instructor. 'The Provo's believe they are calling the shots in the IED game; however we know we have the skills, the intel, and the equipment to show them otherwise; we are no longer playing catch-up.'

We were told we'd all been given the green light to work as search operatives; we'd done a good job; to remember what we had been taught and to take care.

That night we went out and in great RE tradition celebrated by getting plastered.

Wednesday morning we signed over our bedding, got the duty truck to the station and headed back to Cold War Germany.

That was it; Luton – flight - bus and Osnatraz.

Op Banner training and Denmark

The date was Thursday April 18th we were back on parade and our training for Op Banner continued with daily trips to Sennelager.

Fred passed on the news that our misdemeanour with the gnome had returned to Germany with us and the section would carry out a week of guard duty when Sixteen's turn came round again early in May. I was called-out and told to go and see Ron Moody.

Ron presented me with my signing on papers... now I'm pretty convinced this would not happen today, but as I've already written, I was only seventeen and seven months when I arrived in Germany, two months younger still when I passed out of Dover. Adult service began at eighteen; I served eight months in the army in total that was basically unaccounted for and I'm sure I wasn't the only one. I don't believe they even paid us the adult soldiers wage, we were still paid as juniors until we signed on the dotted line at eighteen. Also we were never offered an opportunity to leave the service on moving from Junior to Senior Service. The time we had signed on for in our local information office at fifteen and sixteen years old began from our eighteenth birthday; no option to quit. So the two years we done at Dover never counted toward our service and I find out now forty six years later, at sixty years old, that it doesn't count toward the AFP75 either (that's the armed forces pension 1975). What a typical bloody cop-out by the ministry of prize assoles. Sorry – a soap-box moment, I'll climb down...

Anyway Ron pushed the papers toward me, I sat down on the end of Kev's desk, he showed me where to sign and signed away (for a second time) six years of my life to the Sappers. I'm sure I questioned this at the time but hey... what could Ron tell me other than, 'well that's how it is Steve.'

The daily fitness regime had continued in our absence with some form of activity most mornings and twice a week in the afternoons. Visits to the ranges at Vorden were frequent, live firing SLR and SMG which I really enjoyed and where I could still brag-off my shooting skills.

Officers in Ulster would be issued the Browning 9mm pistol, and it was also being considered that the search team drivers were also issued with a pistol; Reg - three sections driver, John from two section and I thought this was really cool. We ended up being

MQD Form 4A

MEMORANDUM

To ic FD. SGN. Re
3rPo 36

From

Ref. 23/AD P/bon

BRIGHTON

Date 5 Jul 74

Tel. 66688   Ext. 106

Subject   24251061 SGR BuRT. S. J.

Ref A: RemRoi 09·44/74 dated 2 MAY 74
ANNEX B PARA 3 (2)(a).

1. The Sn elected to complete his engagement
on At BERRS signed 18 APR 74 his RoD
is now 3 APR 80. as required by Ref A.

2. On inspection of Part 2 Orders these details
do not appear to have been published
so they have been input into his computer
2O5 by this office.

3. As Part 2 Orders cease to be published from
1 Jul 74. Sn BuRT's Af B2672 should
be amended according to para 1 above.

Rank/
Appointment   SO   Name in
block letters   E ADAMS   Signature

Complete this form in manuscript unless there are special reasons for typing.

Dd. 910378 565249 7/71 B.& S. Ltd.

Note from me...
After signing on my documents should have been sent on to records...
Someone, who will remain nameless forgot to send them. This was the
follow-up memo. Why always me?

issued with an SMG not a pistol when we got to Ballykelly, but we had great fun training and practicing with the pistol on the barrack thirty meter range prior to departure.

A further pastime had been added to our cinema and pub crawling itinerary...

Swimming – the weather was improving; Roberts Barracks had a smashing outdoor pool a stone's throw across the square next to 37 Squadron block (as it was in my time) and it had been filled ready for the summer but at this point in time; outdoor and unheated it took a brave soul to use it. *(The photo of the pool is more a photo of a tree but it's probably the only one in existence. When I returned to Roberts barracks in the summer of 2007 the Sapper Sergeant who walked round with me never even knew there had been a pool or a church in the barrack, however the outline of the pool still remained in the grass).*

The swimming pool in Roberts Barracks.

We were discussing using it one morning at break when one of the Pads mentioned a large pool complex at Dodesheide where he took his kids. His information took the majority of us new boys who'd arrived during the autumn and the winter of the previous year by surprise; we hadn't even heard of it. The Nettebad complex was on Vehrter Landstrasse only a mile from the barracks. It was huge, plush and spotless with two big outside pools plus a diving pond with a spring board as well as a 3,5 and 7 meter boards. There were two indoor pools, one an Olympic size competition pool and a fun pool with a toddler section. A big restaurant overlooked the competition pool. Over the coming three years the Nettebad went a long way in keeping some of us away from continual nights boozing in the Squadron or NAAFI bar. It took about 15 minutes to walk there and a three hour session was next to nothing, five bucks I seem to remember, about a quid. We'd round the evening off with a schnitzel, poms and beer in the restaurant before walking back. The following two summers of 75 and 76 were set to be extremely hot throughout Europe; we'd spend all our spare time at either the barrack pool or at the Nettebad.

On the mornings we never had a physical training session we would leave early to Sennelager, some days in the section Land Rover others by truck, depending on what we were doing. Fitness, shooting, Sappers skills refresher, lectures on future tasking in the province and Sennelager were now our constant routine.

As we approached the beginning of May orders informed us that a Troop from the Squadron were needed for a Nato exercise in Denmark, this was an unexpected turn of events due to our NI commitment; these type of speciality exercises would not normally be on the agenda so close to deployment to Ulster.

The three field sections and the drivers however were made-up adhoc from all four of our Troops, including HQ Troop. We had drivers and wagons from 43 Field Support trucking up the bridging equipment, bar-mine layers and pallets of bar mines. On top of this we also had our Squadron REME (Royal Electrical Mechanical Engineers) support with their 434, a beefed up version of our section 432.

(FV434 Maintenance Carrier. Designated the FV434, this model is used mainly to change major components in the field, such as the complete power-pack of the Chieftain MBT. (Main Battle Tank).There is a crane on the right side of the vehicle which has a lifting capacity of 3,050 kg. The suspension of the FV434 can be locked when the crane is being used. The vehicle has a crew of four. Info courtesy of inetres.com).

Basically it was the close support break-down wagon; the REME guys who were a good bunch of lads, would sort out minor problems on the spot. They would also be accompanying us on Op Banner.

From One Troop there was Ray, Flash Hall, Ginge Vickery, Glenn Scarborough, Nobby Clarke, Titch Graham and Paddy Holmes. Keith Bedwell was to drive the G10 wagon. I was to drive one of the two personnel trucks returning to Traz almost immediately - as in the following day.

The exercise would begin with a briefing in Randers a few miles from the Baltic coast up the Randers Fjord on the east coast of Denmark. APCs would be delivered by rail-flatbed directly to the training area north of Esbjerg on the west coast, as would some bridging parts, bar-mine layer and any other large equipment. Personnel would be driven up by truck, four RLs in total including the G10 wagon, fuel wagon and two trucks that would return after delivering the men. Since January a number of our old Bedford RLs had been replaced with the new MK; for the wheeled vehicle drivers in the MT section it was as if we'd had a second Christmas; in comparison to the RL the MK was a Rolls Royce in both comfort and handling. However for the Squaddie in the back nothing much changes, two rows of slatted seats hooked over the side panels and a canvas hood over the top. Those in the back had a pretty uncomfortable ten hour trip ahead of them.

Oddly our APCs and Ferrets were not loaded onto the flatbeds over the back in the main garrison stores area; they were loaded at the main railway station in town.

This took place on the Wednesday prior to our departure north on the following day. The two previous days had been taken up with fitting of radio sets, loading of section equipment and preparation. I of course along with Alfie Ellis would be coming back after dropping the men in Randers.

I wasn't involved with the loading of the APCs. Each driver and commander took their vehicle into town to the main Banhof rail sidings and drove them onto the flatbeds.

This had proved to be a bit of a spectacle for the German civilian population of the town. The locals living in the rural areas around the garrison towns of Germany were well used to seeing convoys of British military vehicles ploughing through their villages and along their narrow roads. Truth was they were none too happy about it either. However to those in the larger towns or cities it was a bit of a novel event and the loading in the centre of Osnabruck attracted quite a crowd of spectators.

The following morning all tanked up and rearing to go, we had the wagons and one Land Rover for our Troopy lined up in front of the block. Keith drove an MK with the G10 stores, the cook, food and all the gear for 'messing' in the field. Alfie and I drove an MK each with guys and gear in the back. Another wagon had Jerry-cans of fuel for use on the journey up and for refuelling during the exercise.

I had Staff Sergeant Paddy McIntyre in the passenger seat. Titch in the Land Rover with Lieutenant Dixon two troop's boss who would be our boss for just short of two weeks. The idea was to drive north in convoy across the border into Denmark arriving in Randers that evening. Friday would be exercise briefing, the lads would have the weekend free in Randers and Monday truck to Esbjerg, collect their vehicles and deploy into the exercise area. Our surplus men and vehicles, of which I was one, would drive back to Traz the following day until it was time to return and collect the troop for the return journey. As a returning driver I had taken only my overnight stuff and had not drawn a weapon.

Paddy Mac jumped in beside me. 'Morning Burt.'

'Morning Staff.'

'Change of plan Burt; you got three minutes back upstairs grab as much as you need for a couple of weeks in Denmark. Bedwell's coming back, you're staying – questions later, get going and make it sharp.'

Fucking hell, this was bloody typical army!

I jumped down dashed upstairs and jammed anything I could think of into my kit bag including webbing. Back down stairs, Paddy Mac was stood next to the Land Rover talking to Lieutenant Dixon through the window. He saw me appear.

'Ready Burt? Good lets go,' he said without waiting for my reply.

Dixon led the way, blue flag flying; I brought up the rear, green flag on a pole taped to my wing mirror. We were off and I was going to do my first exercise with BAOR in Denmark. Bring it on!

It was a long journey and a long day, six hundred kilometres or four hundred miles at 50mph. We joined the east west Autobahn at Lotte on the south west side of town; the E30 for a couple of miles before turning north on the E37; from here it was almost a straight run north - Bremen, Hamburg, Flensberg, Vejle and Randers, with a stop every couple of hours. Of course we had our brown issue food bags for the journey - a tepid can of drink with an unknown name, curl-cornered corn-dog sannie in white bread (not guaranteed mould free), packet of crisp and a piece of fruit... how wonderfully they look after us.

Randers barracks 74. Danish soldiers scanning the quad for a lost hair clip.

On arriving we were guided into the barrack to the north of the town by a Danish jeep that had been sent to keep an eye out for us.

The barracks in which we were staying were built at the end of World War Two when the old Thorsgrade Barracks in the centre of town, built in 1880, was turned into a council run nursing home. The new barracks were occupied by the Jutland Military Engineers who made us very welcome.

The barracks were modern red brick built in squares with a grassed area in the middle. The rooms were spacious; we slept in bunk beds for the three nights we were there. We ate in the cookhouse with the Danish soldiers who in the main seemed to be conscripts with hair down to their shoulders. The food was good as I remember; one thing about squaddies, regardless of Regiment or Corp a soldier always seems to remember which barracks or camp has the good, bad or indifferent food. Good cooks and chefs are famous and each Squadron tries to get that particular chef attached for field exercises. This I would find out over the coming couple of weeks while working with a young cook who had only just finished training. Poor lad was in for a hard time.

I remember in the cookhouse they had fresh milk that we didn't have in Roberts. The conscripts, when walking around the camp, would pull from his pocket, a 'days to do' yoyo tape and yoyo it up and down. Each day they would cut off a centimetre, which represented a day. The shorter the tape the less time he had left to serve in the army. The guys with short tapes always looked happy.

Ken, Flash, Titch, Tom Ray and Me
Pre-Ex. Randers barrack room 1974

Thing was they just didn't want to be in the army...

On the Friday Alfie and Keith returned to Traz while the rest of us spent the day being briefed on how the exercise would unravel.

Our hosts had arranged for us to go on a sight-seeing tour on the Saturday, which included a military museum, a castle and a tour of the local brewery, this by all accounts was a tradition that had gone on for years when Sappers had come up to Randers for this exercise; this time was no exception. A visit to the Thor Brewery was arranged for us. We were shown around to see the various processes. The visit would conclude with a meal and the tasting of the various beers they brewed. *(Thor was eventually taken over by Royal Unibrew)*.

Friday night we stayed in the Barrack but Saturday night we hit the town and found a club called the 'Cowboy', it was done out in a wild west theme and the seats at the bar were saddles. All the seats and tables were numbered and each table had a phone, there were also phones along the bar. So if you wanted to dance with someone sitting on a table along from you, or you fancied asking them outside for a fag, snog or shag, which for a squaddie - especially a Sapper squaddie was not unheard of; you could phone the table and ask to speak to the girl or boy (not that I'm implying that any of us were after a boy... at least I don't think so?) in number seat so-n-so; or I suppose just say 'could I talk to the blonde lass with the red top', quote clothing or hair colour; I'm sure you get my drift. Everyone was very friendly and in no time we had a table full of girls. It soon became obvious why – the beer – well drinks in general, were an astronomical price and our delectable Danish companions demanded some form of compensation for being our hostesses. It turned out to be a very expensive evening, but not without its rewards, as I found out as the evening wore on and Helga, a girl who'd attached herself to me got ever more tipsy...

A rousing cheer was given to me when 'Helga from the north' and I nipped outside for a quick horizontal tango over the front of a VW beetle in an alleyway behind the club; best investment return on a couple of bottles of Thor Lager ever! This moment springs to mind every time I hear the record 'You're Gorgeous' by Babybird...

For the rest of the week the lads gave me a right ribbing at scoff time - 'hope you've washed your hands' and 'don't let the scabs fall in the stew' y'know good squaddie humour... little did they know what would happen later in the week; but I'll come to that in a couple of paragraphs.

Sunday we stayed in bed late (that was us lads in the barracks, not me and Helga) and spent the rest of the day mooching around the town. That was our taste of Randers and Denmark; Monday morning we'd be up early and with a large contingent of Danish Sappers hit the road to Esbjerg.

This was a NATO exercise, participation was Danish, German, American and British. The training area is/was to the north of Esbjerg and to the west of the village of Oksbol. In the 1960s a large expropriation was carried out, which among others affected 60 farms and 42 permanent habitations. (For the non-Sappers among my readers who struggle over 'expropriation', that word means 'being forcibly moved') Many of the properties are/were still present and a part of the military training area – during our time there the training area covered approximately 10,000 hectare (dune, moor, marsh and forest) which in actual fact, although it sounds it, isn't all that large an area.

Steve with his MK. Pre-exercise Denmark 1974

There was nothing really memorable about this exercise; it seemed to take an age to get going. We drove to Esbjerg and picked up the APCs from the flatbeds; from here we left in convoy for the training area approx. ten miles to the northwest. We drove off the main, and then the side roads into heathland, stopped and parked up; I say parked up because we were still non-tactical and literally just parked in lines against a wood-line. Here we stayed for a further 24 hours before moving into our first harbour area.

Our troop role consisted of bar mine laying, bridge build in support of an attack, and a dismantling job when the tide turned against us. We moved location a couple of times during the exercise but it was all pretty laid back.

I'm guessing the overall objective was to practice working smoothly with our NATO allies.

My job as G10 driver and general dogs-body changed dramatically when the cook was threatened with multiple forms of slow death by the lads due the standard of scoff he was turning out. The first lunch he produced was tomato ketchup sandwiches... need I say more. The troop strung him up to the branch of a tree by his ankles and threatened him with multiple torture if his standards didn't improve. He, the cook, was frightened to death of the Hydroburner and couldn't budget the food allocation. Paddy Mac asked me to do what I could to help and I basically ended up running the cooking while the boy from the ACC (Catering Corp) done as I told him. I found myself playing a prominent role in menu planning and food preparation. How I suddenly required this ability to cook for thirty five blokes in the field having only ever seen it done once on the FFR deployment a few months earlier I really don't know; but I did and I believe I came out of the week a bit of a hero.

I was bored; the guys were going off night and day carrying out Engineer tasks for the battle group, meanwhile I was stuck kicking my heels in the harbour area watching the cook peel spuds; so I asked Paddy Mac if I could be involved in something other

Denmark 74 - Flash, the slightly smarter of the two... as in appearance; with Ginge wearing his Sunday best plus Korean parka top-coat.

than cooking, after all I was a Sapper not a member of the ACC. So one night he gave me the opportunity of going out on a recce with one of the lance jacks; we had a grid reference to make for and had to recce an area of deep ditches for tank crossing Fascine's.

This was more like it and it took me back to my Dover days and the patrols we'd practice night after night in Courses three and seven. We were carrying out this recce right on our enemy's door step, stealth was imperative. So cammed up with just belt kit and weapon we worked our way to the grid reference slowly using good field craft; it was as black as pitch, no moon and cloud obscuring any stars.

We arrived at the grid location and carried out the recce, basically recording the depth and width of the ditches, the composition of the soil on the embankments and any obstructions or abnormalities that would hinder the advance. As our attacking tank force was made up of a couple of Squadrons of British Chieftain's I didn't believe the odd bush or tree would make much difference.

Recce completed we started back, as per standard procedure using a different route then the one taken on the outward leg.

We'd done a mile or so when we came to a churned up area of heathland with loads of big bushes and trees; as we moved slowly forward across this blacked-out landscape a fucking great bush came to life only meters away from us. I almost shit myself; it was the engine of a bloody great German Bundeswehr Leopard tank. These were not bushes; we were slap-bang in the middle of a cammed up tank Squadron. We both froze...

'Bloody hell,' whispered Des (Des being once again a substitute name) 'we're in the middle of a bloody tank Squadron, act natural.'

Act natural..? What he meant I found out later was more a case of acting as though you belong.

We must have somehow, without realizing the fact, stumbled into an enemy harbour area. We'd gone past their guard without being seen - not impossible he may have gone for a leg, a dump, a brew or fallen asleep on the job. Anyway we made like a tree and got out of there pronto... (If you're scratching your head over that one – Biff, Back To The Future, the milk bar scene).

Clearing the enemy area we were making good time keeping to the side of a track when we came upon a farm house, it seemed as we drew close to be in complete darkness; was it occupied, and by who was the question? Taking no chances we continued to slowly by-pass the place keeping in the shadows. We were right opposite the front door when the lights of a vehicle came up the road, not head lights – side lights. We knew then whoever was driving was being tactical. Both of us simultaneously jumped from the kerb side into the ditch.

Peering over the edge we watched as an American Jeep stopped outside the front door; an American soldier got out and knocked. The door opened and a conversation took place on the step. This was the enemy; the Yanks and Krauts against us and the Danes.

Obviously the driver never expected to go inside as the engine of the jeep was still running. Des and I watched and waited; it was late and we were knackered but we couldn't move until either the guy went inside or left. Also we couldn't see either of the people clearly as there was no light behind the person in the hall; the hall or room behind them was in darkness. Suddenly the person on the step moved forward and the door closed. The jeep was left with no one in it and the engine running.

'Come on,' said Des, 'let's go.'

'No Des,' I replied, 'let's nick the jeep, why walk when we can drive home? We got a map, we know where we are, let's drive back.'

'No we're not doing that, we'll be right in the shit,' was Des reply.

'Oh for Christ-sake don't be such a woose Des, we're on exercise, they're the enemy, he should have known better - come on lets drive it away.'

But no Des wouldn't do it...

'Well at least let's have a look and see if there's anything nickable.' I said; I was exasperated... this was a golden opportunity going to waste.

Before he could say another word I was up, and in a crouching run, keeping the jeep between me and the house, dashed across the road. A quick look inside showed me that the soldier, whoever he was had left everything in the jeep including his weapon. I just grabbed it and ran back.

'Come on Des lets go,' I urgently whispered and without stopping made my way straight into the undergrowth. Des was right behind me.

'What the fuck are you doing,' he was saying. 'What you got there? You haven't nicked his weapon fur Christ sake have you? You fucking idiot, the shit will really be on our heads; stop for Christ sake we got to take it back.'

But I wasn't stopping; we had a couple of miles to go and there was no way I was taking the Armalite (M16) back. We could still see the house behind us and I wanted to put some distance between it and us.

Eventually we found a place to stop and rest.

'You bloody idiot Burt' (it was Burt now not Steve; rank superiority). 'What the fuck are you doing? I'm washing my hands of this, I'll tell Lieutenant Dixon you totally disobeyed my order not to go to the jeep.'

'No I didn't; you ordered me not to nick the jeep - you never stopped me from going to look inside it and you never told me not to come back with spoils. Fucking hell Des, what was the first thing you learnt about your weapon? Never leave the bloody thing unattended, take it with you everywhere you go – scoff, bed, shitter eh? So this tosser loses his weapon and we claim it; tough on him, we'll see what Paddy Mac says. Now get the bloody map out and let's get going I'm dying for a brew.'

Des said no more, he figured out the route without my help in a churlish way and just got up and moved out. It took us just over an hour to get back to our harbour area a ramshackle mix of old farm buildings. The guard challenged us through and we went to the cammed up troop commanders APC, to report to Lieutenant Dixon and Paddy Mac.

I stood behind Des and heard him say, 'we're back Staff, we got the gen but first I think Burt's got something to tell you. You may not be too pleased.'

Burt's got something to tell you Staff, you may not be to pleased – snivelling git.

'Oh? What's the problem Burt?' Des stood to one side... *Lieutenant Dixon must be getting his head down.*

Fuck it, I thought, in for a penny eh?

'Well Staff; I brought this back,' I said thrusting the Armalite in front of me.

'Bloody hell!' Said Staff McIntyre.'

'Interesting.' Said Lieutenant Dixon, having awoken and peering out of his sleeping bag at the end of the APC bench seat... and prey tell Burt what lorry did this fall off the back of?

'Well Sir, Staff, it was left unattended in the back of a jeep...'

And so I told the story, leaving out the bit where Des was so negative. I thought if he wanted to say something about it he would.

'Right lets debrief first, then the Armalite story.' Ordered Dixon.

We both sat in the back of the APC while Des recounted the recce and consulted his notes. He continued on up to the point where I ran to the jeep. At that point I had to interrupt and say that I was not ordered not to go to the jeep, only that I shouldn't steal it.

'Ok Corporal leave it with us; get yourself a brew if you want one and get your head down, your section's in the field in a couple of hours and you'll be with them. I'll discuss this M16 business with Burt.'

Des left us.

'Burt,' Staff McIntyre began, 'I see your reasoning behind taking this unattended weapon. Whoever it belongs to shouldn't have walked off leaving it in his vehicle. Worse still he went into the house and closed the door with the engine running: In our army his feet - if caught, wouldn't touch the ground on the way to the 'nick' but he's a Sherman and they run with different rules... now... did you consider the fact - no you didn't, that stealing the weapon would indicate the presence of an enemy? That you may have been hunted down and captured? The implications of which I don't need to spell out to you... do I? This was impetuous Burt you need to think things through before doing something like this; if it had gone wrong it could have jeopardised tomorrow night's attack. You carried out enough patrol training at Dover to know a reconnaissance patrol is all about stealth. Getting in and getting out without the enemy knowing you've been there. You understand where I'm coming from don't you? It was not your job to make a fool out of a Yank soldier; your job was to bring back information.

'Yes Staff,' I said. I was disappointed...

'Go on get out of here I'm sure the shit will hit the fan and in a couple of hours, we'll be crawling with umpires making enquiries about a missing weapon and no, the Yank should never have left his weapon unattended; I'm sure he'll never do it again. Leave it to me, I'll deal with it Sir,' he said to Lieutenant Dixon whilst holding out his hand for the weapon.

I handed it over.

'Where's the magazine?'

'Wasn't one Staff.'

Both Dixon and Paddy Mac were turning the M16 over and having a good look.

'Apparently these are crap; jam up with the smallest grain of mud or sand... Light though, a hell of a lot lighter than our SLR and they have an automatic mode... Whoever lost this is in for a bollocking I'll bet.

Go and get yourself a brew Burt and get your head down. We'll try and avoid any flak from this and Lieutenant Dixon and I will decide whether you need more than just a verbal bollocking over this later.'

'It'll be ok, Paddy Mac will sort it,' I said to Des as we met again in the ruined stable that acted as the field kitchen. But I never told him everything Paddy Mac had said to me.

Des never replied but from that moment on we were never on good terms.

The tea urn was sitting there for whoever wanted a brew. The cook was curled up in his sleeping bag in the corner on a pile of old hay. I gave him a shake with my boot; it was past four and there was no way I'd be helping him with the breakfast, I wanted to sleep on as long as I could.

'Oy,' I said sticking my boot on the sleeping bag. 'Wake up.'

A head came out of the bag.

'What time is it? Is it time to get breakfast?'

'No it fuckin well isn't – listen; it's gone four and I'm just back. I'm getting some kip so get the food sorted on your own in the morning; don't wake me unless it's a bloody emergency.' Without waiting for his answer headed for my sleeping bag in the back of the MK.

Someone was shaking me… I opened very tired eye's to see Flash Hall the command vehicle driver? 'What time is it Flash?'

'It's eight mate, get up – you've caused a right fucking hooha nicking that weapon. Paddy Mac wants to see you right now.'

Oh shit here we go… and I thought I'd got off lightly.

I climbed out of my bag, put on my boots, putees, wooly-pully and cap; grabbed my weapon and went over to the command APC; Staff McIntyre was inside with the radio operator a lad called Matt Whittaker. No sign of Lieutenant Dixon or the other APCs. I must have slept the sleep of the dead, I didn't hear them leave.

'Morning Staff - you wanted me?'

'Morning Burt, trust you slept well?' This was said in a kind of sarcastic tone with the hint of a smile. I wondered what was coming…

'Yes Staff, thanks…'

'Good; because while you've been off in the land of fucking nod we've had to explain away your actions of last night; by actions I mean the taking of that bloody weapon. By the time you'd got your head down this morning the airwaves were full of news regarding a missing M16. We – as in the exercise participants from Sixteen Squadron had to admit to having it and the reason why. And I can tell you, the owners were not amused and did not believe they were in any way in the wrong leaving it in the jeep. If that's the way they run their show that's up to them, but we don't; so I told them no action would be taken against you and they ought to be more careful with their weapon security. That didn't go down well either – fuckin Yanks. However Lance Corporal *** is not amused and accused you of breaking his order? What have you got to say to that?'

I didn't Staff; as I said last night, I wanted to steal the whole jeep and Corporal *** said no. He said nothing about anything else.'

'But he told you to put it back?'

Yes Staff but that wasn't possible, there wasn't time and by the time he said it we were already a half a klick away from the house. We'd been caught if I'd gone back.'

'You're to bloody sharp for your own good Burt, I let you off the lead for two hours and you cause an international incident - go on, clear off and get some scoff; oh! And have a wash as well.' *Of course I was still covered in cam-cream.*

I departed for the sheep shed wondering if this would go further...

Paddy Mac along with Fred Ludlow and Mick Dobson had all been 'B' and 'C' Squadron SNCO instructors at Dover, they were well aware of the type of kids that had gone through Old Park Barracks; let's be honest, you had to be a certain type of kid to leave home at fifteen years old and sign up for the army; confident, self-assured and resourceful; these attributes were turned into the leadership qualities that the Corps of Royal Engineers were looking for; kids who could use there initiative and resourcefulness. But at times that cockiness could go a step to far as it had with me that night in Denmark.

At least our ex-Dover SNCOs knew what the ex-boy soldiers were like and I believe they cut us some slack. However Staff McIntyre was right; I'd acted without thinking, hadn't listened to Des and in truth been a bit of a jumped up know all. Here was a lesson to be learnt.

Breakfast had finished, however our cook, indebted to me for his life earlier in the exercise had kept me back some tinned sausage and tinned tomatoes; there was bread and also fresh eggs.

Hot water as usual was permanently bubbling in a Dixie. I thought I'd wash before having my scoff so went to the wagon to collect a bowl for water. *There is an art-form to washing in the field. Water is precious and needs to be used sparingly for the different things you need it for. My routine was given to me by others who had more experience. If I had a couple of litres of water. First I'd clean my teeth using a handful of water to swill my mouth out and rinse the brush. Putting the toothbrush to one side and using a flannel I'd wash face, neck and (not every day) nether's.*

Left with a grubby bowl of water I'd use it to rinse out my socks or a pair of pants which would dry on the top of the engine.

I took my mess tins and went back to the sheep shed for food.

'Right carry on this morning while you were sleeping,' the young cook said. 'You stole a rifle from some American jeep last night? He was looking at me as if he couldn't believe anyone would be so stupid.

'Yeah, well he shouldn't've left it lying around should he; his own bloody fault. Why? What went on this morning exactly?'

'The umpires turned up first, they only beat the Yank by a couple of minutes... he was angry; they were round the back of the APC but everyone could hear what was going on. He, the Yank, said this was an exercise not war and you shouldn't have taken it, rules are different on exercise. Lieutenant Dixon outranked the Yank so he didn't seem that bothered; he said No; any exercise is training for the real thing and wouldn't expect any of his men to go anywhere without his weapon. Said he admired the tenacity of his soldier and would not be reprimanding you. Then he asked them to leave. He could do that I suppose because the Yank was only a second Lieutenant – single bronze bar. The radio op said the Umpires never got involved, never said anything; they were Danes.'

'So was it the Yank officer's weapon then?' I asked.

'Yeah, I guess so; everyone was having breakfast, they all heard it; thought it was hilarious. Didn't you hear the guys cheering as he drove off?'

'No I was sleeping the sleep of the dead; to be honest I'm glad I missed it.'

Later the field sections returned and I had to run through my story a few times while dishing out scoff. I kept it down though; I thought it best that the incident blow over as soon as possible. What I didn't want was for the rumblings to continue after we got back and have to answer more questions from Bill Dunn, the 2I/C or God forbid our OC. Least said, soonest mended as they say.

That evening was our last in the field before moving into a debriefing area for the following morning. We would eat our final meal in the old sheep shed. The troop would then head out on a final task and the remainder of the vehicles would make for the final location.

We - the cook and I were pretty glad to hear that breakfast would be prepared by a central Danish army field kitchen the following morning. We had exhausted almost all our rations. We had tinned tomatoes, powdered egg and powdered mash to prepare the dregs for the last meal.

As it got dusk the lads were de-camming ready for the off while the cook and I emptied gallon cans of tomatoes into a Dixie and boiled water for the powdered scrambled egg and mash. It was quite dark in the shed; light was provided by the flame of the Hydro-burner and a couple of Tillie lights. The windows had been blacked out with empty ration boxes and a canvas tilt covered the entrance. I was moving Dixie's one by one so water and food came to the boil simultaneously when I stepped back kicking over the Dixie of tomatoes!

(What follows happened a long time ago, in early May 1974, forty four years ago to be exact and I've never told a soul about it. Even at reunion under the plied pressure of beer I've never let-on the story of the 'Herb's'. But now the truth is about to be disclosed).

'Bloody hell,' shouted the cook.' You've kicked over the tomatoes!'

He didn't need to tell me I could see a hundred tomatoes and all the juice escaping and being absorbed into the dried sheep shit on the floor.

'Shut up for Christ sake!' I said. 'Keep your bloody voice down you'll have every bugger in here. Get the big ladles and let's get the fucking things back in the Dixie.'

'You can't put them back in the Dixie, you can't dish them up they're floating in sheep shit.' Wailed the whimp of a cook.

193

'Yes we can, we've sod all else to feed them with, come on shift yourself and let's see what happens.'

Using ladles and spatula's we got all the tomatoes and seventy five percent of the juice back into the Dixie and slowly it reheated; however on the top was an inch of dried sheep shit, floating around like an alien crustacean. The cook looked into the pot... 'No, no, no, I'm not being a party to this, you'll poison the whole troop and I'll get the blame, they'll kill me again.'

'Shut the fuck up, there's nothing wrong with it – watch.' Slowly I skimmed, what now resembled dried grass, from the top of the Dixie and flicked it into the far recesses of the barn. Bit by bit the juice in the Dixie cleared and I added some hot water to replace the juice that had been lost on the floor and absorbed into the dried, what I will now refer to as hay.

'There you are, see what I mean... no one will ever know unless you say something and if you say something it'll be me that kills you. I've done you more than one favour this week mate; it's now pay back time. Got it?'

He peered into the Dixie. 'I guess you wouldn't know... eh?' He said dubiously.

'Right,'. 'Let's skim as much of this crud off the top as we can and call the lads in for scoff. Act normal and if anyone says anything they're herbs ok? For fuck sake don't say anything else.'

We called the lads through. They all tucked in and seemed to enjoy it; only one or two commented on the little flecks of green floating in the tomato juice which of course were herbs from a batch of tinned tomatoes with herbs and spices, courtesy of the civilian Compo supplier. When your life depends on it you're best just to look the person in the eye and be unwavering in your story telling.

Grub consumed the guys had their brew and one by one the three APCs moved out for their last night of tasking. Those of us left behind cleared up, packed up and headed into the night toward our last non-tactical harbour area where we would meet with the Yanks, Danes and German Bundeswehr.

Our final nights harbour area was the same location we'd sat in during the first 24 hours before the exercise started over a week ago. We arrived, reversed the command vehicle and our other couple of trucks into position and got our heads down for the night.

In the morning the whole troop was together again; plus two wagons that had come up from Traz.

The Danes had set up a communal field kitchen, a communal field shower tent and latrines which consisted of a long pole over a ditch supported by cross bracings at either end. It has been the only time in my life when I've used a latrine such as this, there was no avoiding it. If you wanted a crap it was pants down and join another five or six guys with your ass hanging over a ditch on a pole. The paper roles were stuck over 6 inch nails every metre along the pole, and a second pole prevent a person from falling backwards into the ditch. I wish that at the time I'd had the foresight to have my camera with me and take a picture of what was a truly unbelievable sight. But hey who takes their camera to the bog with them...

Whatever was supposed to happen between the officers happened and by mid-morning we were heading for the goods yard at Esbjerg station and loading the tracked vehicles onto the flatbeds; in the afternoon once again in convoy we headed across country through Ribe and Gram joining the E45 south at Roekro. It was a long journey back to Osnabruck and we arrived back in the early hours of the morning. I was grateful that on the return I had Paddy Holmes in the passenger seat rather than Paddy Mac, so no more questions about the Armalite.

On arrival at Roberts' the wagons were parked overnight outside the block; the armoury was opened for the handing in of weapons and we hit the sack.

The one thing that stands out in my mind from the return journey was our arrival at the Danish, German border at Ellund. Of course this was in the days of proper borders and proper Custom posts; as well as the Customs there was an autobahn service's where we had a coffee.

But there was also a shop totally devoted to pornography. Honest, I tell you no lie. Now, sex shops were non-existent in the UK apart from a few sleazy back street or ally shops with blacked out windows. They were not uncommon in the red light districts of German towns but this one, wow! Very modern looking and very large on the border crossing was like a supermarket compared to a corner shop. The variety of magazines alone was mind boggling. Of course we didn't go in did we... we just took a quick glance through the window.

Munster Missile Site and advance party warning

Over the following few days the normal post exercise wind-down took place. Tracked vehicles were collected from the town Banhof, stores and radios handed in, Weapons cleaned and vehicles washed down. Life for those not involved with Denmark had meant weapons training, live firing at Vorden, Tin City and fitness. We - those of us that had had a couple of weeks respite in Demark, would also be back on the treadmill leading up to Op-Banner. There were no repercussions from the Armalite incident; Lt Dixon and Paddy Mac must have decided to let it go; which was bloody decent of them.

I took a long weekend at home at the end of May; I caught the train for Osnabruck through to Hook of Holland on a Friday night, the bank holiday weekend; caught the boat to Harwich where dad picked me up in the car. It was good to see my family again, although with the courses I'd done over the preceding months I'd seen them quite frequently since the New Year. The car and passenger ferry's on this route ran far more frequently in the seventies, the early boat leaving at eight in the morning for the seven hour crossing, then another early afternoon and a night boat leaving at 10pm.

The talk at home during the weekend revolved around my forthcoming tour in Northern Ireland; the civil unrest. Bombings and shootings at this point were really at an all-time peak with constant news coverage on the TV; internment was the big issue – locking people up for an indefinite period without trial, was incredibly controversial and prompted riots all over the province on a daily basis. As the year wore on this would get worse and prompt serious outbreaks of rioting in both the Maze and Magilligan prisons; incidents of the future that our Squadron would be involved with.

Both my parents were worried sick and just didn't see me as a warrior for my country but as someone just out of short pants. To be totally honest I really did only look about fifteen and only shaved once a week. I daren't tell them that I was going to be involved with searching out hidden explosive devices... that news would have taken both of them clear over the edge. I played the whole thing down.

Dad drove me back to Harwich in the early hours of Monday. We came off the A12 at Dedham and headed for Mistley; this was the quickest route before the upgrade to the A120.

The roads were narrow and winding. It was early, with hardly any traffic when we came round a bend to find a serious accident.

A Morris Minor had left the road and rolled a number of times taking out a hedge and coming to a halt in a field. The driver was lying without movement in the ditch that the car had passed over; probably not wearing a seat belt he'd been thrown from the car as it tumbled. Most cars at that time never even had seat belts fitted, only the more expensive manufactures fitted them as standard.

We stopped. We had no first aid kit only some old rags dad kept in the boot; I ran to the guy in the ditch while dad went to check out the car.

It was a man, there was no one in else the car; he was wearing the uniform of a customs officer, he was unconscious but breathing. His forehead was split wide open with blood all over his face. Dad said this has just this moment happened the wheels are still turning on the upturned car.

I told dad to take our car to the nearest house and call an ambulance. I would stay with the man.

Dad shot off and I wrapped rag around the guy's head to stem the flow of blood. There was a bag in the field between me and the car I ran and got it. A normal everyday shopping bag it contained a sandwich box a clean shirt and a towel. I guessed he was on his way to Harwich for a shift at the docks, if this hadn't happened to him he'd have been checking me through customs by now. I used the clean shirt to replace the old rag I'd used on his head. He had a pulse and his breathing was not laboured. I thought the best thing to do was leave him undisturbed and wait.

A couple of cars had stopped, others asking if they could help. I said there wasn't much that could be done, but if anyone had blankets in their car could they get them to throw over the guy and keep him warm. A couple of people said they had dog blankets and ran off to get them. Dad came back he had a women with him, she was a nurse. She said if we wanted to leave she would stay with the guy till the ambulance came. Dad and I checked the time; there was no way we'd make the 8am ferry now so there was no rush. We elected to stay till the police and ambulance turned up. The couple who had provided the blankets said they had to be on their way; coincidentally they'd just got off a ferry in Harwich; don't worry about the blankets they said they are old anyway.

The police got to the scene first, looked at the guy and knew him. They took mine and dads statement which took about fifteen minutes to write, they took our name and address. While this was going on the 'Plod' called in a wreaker truck for the car; the blood wagon arrived. Statement signed dad and I left for Harwich.

Dad dropped me and said goodbye I took my single small bag to a grotty little waiting area where there were a couple of vending machines sat down.

I had a long wait; the next ferry was at 2pm getting in at 10pm local Dutch time. I wasn't overly worried the trains from The Hook met every boat; they ran right through Holland and Germany as far as Berlin without having to change — no, the real pain was having to wait in Harwich six hours.

The boat docked around 10pm and the boat-train as it was called at the time, pulled out of The Hook at 11pm bank holiday Monday 27th May; I was on it and would get off 4 hours later in Traz. I knew by the time I got to bed it would almost be time to get up, I may be lucky and get three hours in the sack.

I wasn't really tired as I'd dozed in a recliner on the ferry crossing so I went to the restaurant/buffet car and ordered a ham omelette and a glass of Amstel.

With a second glass of beer I settled in my seat, read and listened to the rhythm of the train taking me back to Traz...

Someone was shaking my shoulder; I came awake to see the conductor stood over me.

'Osnabruck,' he said.

'Dank u.' (Dutch) Christ that was decent of him, I'd slept through every station on the route and would probably have slept through this one as well if he hadn't woke me.

It was gone 3am when I walked out the station to the taxi rank. Fortunately the clubs and bars stayed open most of the night so as well as trains arriving and departing there were always squaddies looking for a cab back to their barracks.

I had a quick squint at Part 2 orders before going upstairs.

1 Troop with elements of 2 Troop to parade on Friday morning for a seven day detachment for 'Munster site guard' Handorf..? Interesting; what the fucks that all about I wonder? I'd ask Nobby in the morning. Also - Squadron to parade at 1330 in full combats for Pre-Op Banner photo.

I went upstairs and being as quiet as I could be, because I was a decent kind of bloke, shrugged of my clothes and hit the sack for three hours.

Reveille shout was anytime between 0630 and 0700 depending on where the duty screw started and how many people he spoke to on the way round.

He woke us: Eric Brown lent out of bed coughed himself awake and kick started his lungs with a B&H; I followed suit with one of my French Du Maurier cigarettes, my death stick of choice; no one else's I might add, I couldn't give em away...

'You got in late mate,' this from Eric.

So I set about telling him the story of my return journey. Fag finished I went for a wash, got dressed and with Eric wandered over for some Breckie.

'What's the story with this 'Munster guard thing?' I asked him.

'Yeah what a bummer that is, we've a week of that fuckin shit; that's what Munster guard is, bloody awful, I've done it before, it's a pig of a job. We go to a place just east of Munster... there's a couple of places near Munster actually. This time we're at Handorf, the other place is east something... Ostbevern or something like that. It's a crap duty; we're guarding strategic weapons in bunkers for the Sherman's.' They're a bunch of up-their-own-asses pompous bastards, all think their God's gift because their part of a strategic rocket unit; bunch of idiots. Thankfully because of Banner we're only doing a week. The sites are shitoles; we guard the perimeter and man the towers, the Yanks look after the storage areas and inner sanctums. We get bored shitless. You're not supposed to have a book, a magazine or a radio; although guys do smuggle em in. The floors are covered in porno material. Hang on let's get our grub.' We crossed the road heading for the rear door of the cook house - the door that Ginge took me through the night of the cockroach nightmare. This morning, at the end of May the leaves were out on the trees and the sun was shining it was a really lovely morning. Eric and I joined the queue for scoff. A couple of other 1 Troop lads were already in. We took our plates and sat with Stodge, Titch, Derek and Benny. They said hi, how was Blighty?' I said ok... Eric piped up again.

'Steve wants to know about Munster guard...'

'Oh yeah Munster guard mate, something else you've got to look forward to, you'll love this shite. So where do we start... It's a crap duty; everything's shite; the food, the accommodation, the rostering, everything, and just watch what you touch in the towers.' This was Benny and he was laughing...

'What do you mean you got to watch what you touch?'

'Harry Monk mate, it gets everywhere... you'll get guys up there determined to make themselves go blind, anything to relieve the boredom, then smear the left overs on the door handle.'

'Or take the back off the torch and fire off into the working parts; put the battery back in upside down so the lad you hand over too gets a handful when he unscrews the end cap.' Interrupted Derek...

'Or another good one,' chipped in another voice. 'Smear it around the eye piece of the Bino's.'

By now the whole table was laughing, I couldn't believe what I was hearing. 'God that's bloody disgusting.' I said.

'Yeah but well funny,' someone else piped up.

One of the Munster towers.

'That's not all - the towers stink, the accommodation's gross, and the foods crap. The only entertainment is rubbing the Sherman's up the wrong way and watching their fucking antics on an hourly basis. We're issued live rounds as well; stories abound of blokes shooting into the woods just for the hell of it; yeah mate you got it all to look forward to.'

Then they all started telling stories of what had gone on during the site guard... of course they were mainly stories passed on from one unit to another; whether true or not who knows. One such story involved a young Sprog, not a Sapper I might add, who threatened to shoot himself... apparently this lad from some unit or other had a ribbing over a negligent discharge and couldn't bear the slagging he was getting. (That's a negligent from his military weapon not to be confused with anything else!)

When this ribbing continued over the radio he decided to top himself. I think they just got to him in time.'

Someone else on the table piped up - 'The Yanks have these set piece challenges you've got to say as well - something like 'Advance one and be recognised - I recognise you as a member of the on-site guard, advance all'. God what crap. Most of the time the dumps are empty they move the warheads around to different locations. Radio checks every fifteen minutes to Portsmouth barracks.'

'Portsmouth barracks Stevie, that could be you mate... you may get lucky, you're a radio-op aren't you?'

'Yeah... so.'

'Well two radio-ops are based in Portsmouth barracks in Munster. They have a radio check routine every fifteen minutes with the site. But they're stuck in one room with a toaster, after a couple of weeks you're climbing up the walls; I'd rather be on the advance party then in Munster doing that crap...'

'What's a toaster?' I naively asked. I thought it was a nickname for some bit of kit.

The old hands were wetting themselves...

'You know what a bloody toaster is, a bread toaster, the radio ops live all week on toast and marmalade.' Answered Eric; 'What did you think I meant?'

Everyone was laughing.

I left it at that, I didn't really want to know anything else. I'd learnt by now that everything was a wind-up; that the lads loved retelling the most gross and unbelievable stories to the Sprogs of the Squadron; it would be that way till I got some 'time-in' and that 'time-in' was only just a few weeks away.

Site guard? I'd find out for myself soon enough anyway.

We all got up and left for the block.

On parade at 0820 3 Troop were tasked to arrange tables and seats on the square in front of the block for our pre-deployment photograph. We were told to parade in combats.

Not every person in the photo went to Ballykelly; a rear party was left behind of a few guys to keep the Squadron office ticking over, deliver the Pad's mail, and keep our battle wagons in running order.

A present day (2018) satellite view of the remains of the Ostbevern missile site.

After lunch parade in combat dress, we were dismissed and told to size-off for the photo. A photographer came from town to capture us in celluloid; we stood, knelt and sat on the tables, till the photographer had us all positioned and was happy with the shot.

Then followed a speech by the OC; warning us of what was to come. That this imminent tour was a serious active service deployment against an enemy, who, more often than not remained in the shadows. An enemy that had every intension of doing away with any number of us if they were able and we gave them that opportunity.

But he assured us we'd prepared well for the task ahead and how he had every confidence that we would carry out our role diligently and professionally.

This was real soldiering and we would be doing it every day all day and frequently nights, for the next four months.

Following the breakup of the photo Fred grabbed me... 'Burt, report to the Squadron office for your annual confidential. Lt Wray will see you now.'

I made my way into the Block with the other office based personnel and waited outside the Troop office door. Both Fred and Timmy passed me and called me in behind them. 'Come in Burt and take a seat.'

'Thank you Sir,' I said while saluting.

'Well Burt, you've had an interesting seven months with us which hasn't been without its ups and downs. However in the main I believe it's been positive and productive and Staff Ludlow agrees. You've done two courses and the results from both were better than average in fact very good; you conducted yourself well during FFR and you seem to have slotted into the troop well; reports from Staff Scott are also positive regarding your role within the MT. Now, the misdemeanours along the way – you know what they are so I won't go into the detail again; you've hopefully learnt from the different episodes... we all make mistakes from time to time, the idea is to learn from them. (I'm sure he was at this point remembering his own mistake of running naked through the centre of town just before Christmas). You need to rein yourself in Burt, not be so impetuous and think things through before jumping in with both feet. I heard what happened in Demark; that was acting without thinking; during the next four months you'll be doing a job where acting without thinking could quite possibly get you killed. You have a good future ahead of you Burt, slow down, keep out of trouble, keep away from those who will probably not progress up the rank structure and will lead you astray. You were a Junior Leader and the object of your career is in that very name – progress through the ranks and rapidly. I shall write up this report and you will be called back to initial it. One final thing Burt and this will appear on orders this evening. You will be accompanying Corporal

Milton on the advance party to Ballykelly. Now, do you agree with what I've said so that it can be written up on your report?'

'Yes Sir, thank you Sir.'

'Good, anything to add Staff,' said Timmy turning to Fred.

'No sir I think you've covered everything.'

'Excellent, any questions Burt?'

'Well yes Sir just one thing, we were told that we would be receiving danger money for our search team operations; do you know how much this will be?'

No I don't Burt, but I'm sure if you ask Sergeant Moody he'll be able to tell you.'

Period covered by report:

From: **NOV 73** To: **JUN 74**

Rank held and how employed during period

SPR ~ Driver

Assessment of soldier

Sapper Burt is a cheerful young man who has been employed as the GIO?? driver. He has worked very hard and takes pride in his vehicle. He is willing honest and reliable and his turnout is improving.

He has settled with and is a good member of the MT. He has a promising future.

Signature of C.O. or officer under whom employed

Name _WRAY_ Rank _2LT_ Appt. _Tp Commd C_

Date _10 Jan 74_

Initials of soldier and date

17 6 1974

'Thank you Sir.' I stood, saluted and marched out. I turned right and went into Ron's office.

'Hi Sarg, just a quick question.'

'Fire away Burt.'

'This danger money for the search teams... how much is it?'

'You'll not dine out this Burt, unless you save it for the complete tour – the price of a pint in Blighty, thirty five pence a day...'

Fucking tight bastards, life on the line for thirty five pence a day; bloody hell.

'Thanks Sarg, guess we'll just do it for Queen and Country then eh?'

'Best way to view it Steve, you're working for the army mate not nationalized industry.' He said laughing.

I went to ask the other lads in my section if they knew of this colossal sum we were going to be paid. They didn't and the reaction was similar to my own.

Orders appeared regarding the missile site guard. I was not down to take part; however along with the site guard list was posted a list of the advance party to Ballykelly. My name was down for this along with other search team drivers, section Corporals, SQM department headed-up by our QM, Lou Rex; MT office, signals, control room and the armoury staff; around forty personnel in all. We would be leaving in one week.

I needed to find a pen-pal; female obviously. It seems strange now in 2018 that you sat down and wrote to people with a pen on paper; where we now live in an age of texting, emails and telephone. But not in 1974; you wrote; you rarely phoned and if you did it was generally because something was wrong. During my time at Dover I'd written to three girls, Angie my childhood girlfriend. That had ended during my Course seven at Dover. Clare – another girl from Secondary school a relationship that was still going, be it not quite so full-on; she lived in Wiltshire had also left school and was working, so it was hardly surprising that her interest for a soldier in Germany, rarely making an appearance in her life could remain strong. And Monika a German friend of mine who I'd known for years, she lived in Munich, Bavaria; we'd exchange letters three or four times a year.

I needed something closer to my home in Norfolk where I didn't have a single friend male or female. A girl I could catch up with when visiting my parents in the 'Dark Side' as I referred to East Anglia and Norfolk in particularly.

For some time I'd hunted through the Union Jack, Sixth Sense and Forces Echo all squaddie papers of the time to find the right girl in the right location; a girl pen-pal who I could fantasise about while fulfilling my celibate tour of duty in Northern Ireland. (Little did I know at that point in time, just how overrun with girls the next four months were going to be).

I needed a new girl, a girl I could write to pouring out my lonely heart and hopeful shag on R&R.

As odd as it may seem now, girls did look for soldiers, airmen and sailors to write to via these forces papers; a kind of pre on-line dating service...And, believe it or not, there was no shortage of women on offer.

I found mine... age seventeen, dark blonde hair - whatever colour that is, blue eyes and five foot seven. Name of Pru Tinker lives in Newmarket. Please send photo...

Photos exchanged I was more than happy with my acquisition, everything was proportional with no obvious (visible on the photo) deficiencies or extra bits, and so it seemed was she. The correspondence began...

The time had come for the advance party to leave. Over the preceding week, and following 1 Troops return from the Munster guard site, weapons had been crated, the necessary G10 stores that were not waiting for us in Ballykelly were boxed and a mind boggling amount of duty-free spirit purchased from the NAAFI and carefully prepared for transit, ready for use in our own Squadron bar in Ballykelly.

The majority of equipment we required was already 'in theatre' or in layman's terms, already in use by the Squadron we were relieving; permanently housed in the hangers and stores at our location on the airfield. It would be handed over, checked and signed for on arrival by the advance party.

Among these many items were included - Vehicles, G10 items, construction and everyday type building consumables; as well as flak-jackets and of course baton guns and rubber bullet guns.

The advance party, including myself were also in the process of packing - kitbags, large packs and suitcases ready to be trucked to Gutersloh. I took along the brown brick Roberts radio that belonged to Nobby, I told him I'd pay him for it when we got over there, I still owed him for it four months later when we got back.

It was all go and there was an air of anticipation and feel-good about the Squadron. We had been building up to this moment since our speech from the OC at New Year. We wanted to be off – we wanted to get on with it.

We loaded our stores weapons and personal gear onto a fleet of RLs and MKs parked outside the block. Job done we were off to Gutersloh for a Hercules transport to Aldergrove, the main airport north west of Belfast in Northern Ireland.

At Gutersloh all items had to be cross-loaded from the trucks to the Herc; carried out under the watchful eye of Q Rex and the load masters who then secured the boxes to the deck of the plane. At the top of the ramp were two rows of canvas seats facing aft (backwards) these were for us the Sixteen Squadron advance party. Preparations concluded; equipment strapped down, baggage netted to the floor, Sappers in their seats the load master gave us a flight brief.

The ramp came up and we were off to carry out some very serious soldiering.

16 Field Squadron. Pre Op Banner 1974

Epilogue

My initial intention when I started this book was to include my full adult army service within one volume. However it soon became obvious to me that to do so would create a book of so many pages as to make it impractical. I wanted to record all my memories in detail, as I did in 'Boys to Men'; the story of my time in Dover.

If I wrote the whole story - my pre-arrival, my first seven months in Germany - my time in Northern Ireland, and the following two years in BAOR, in one book, this would consist of around a thousand pages.

I made the decision to split the story into three parts based on timings mentioned above.

I would like to remind the reader that this book is written as a personal memoir based entirely on my own experiences and recollections – what my life was like and the things that happened to me personally during my first seven months in Osnabruck.

I enjoyed my time in Sixteen immensely and after returning from Northern Ireland felt a part of the Squadron's senior element, as I suspect did my comrades of a similar age and experience; we – the lads who'd joined in the previous year before Op Banner felt as if we'd earned our spurs so to speak; this was certainly not how I felt before we left on Banner in the June, I still felt very much the new kid on the block.

The first seven months in Sixteen was a steep learning curve; but I never screwed up – the courses, exercises and tasks I was given, I carried out well and achieved good results. My cockiness spilled over in Denmark with the Armalite incident but it taught me a lesson and reigned me in a bit.

I was a very young fresh faced kid when I arrived in Germany. I looked no more than fifteen years old; you've only got to look at me on the cover photo sitting on the Danish truck to see that.

Some may feel it's unfair of me to mention the bullying that went on during my first month by one solitary individual. I make no apologies for including this; it was, and is, a part of my story, it was

211

unpleasant start to life in Sixteen for myself and other young Sappers who'd arrived in the Troop from training Regiments. It was resolved in a short time and as far as I'm aware never reoccurred. It happened, there is no elaboration - in fact if anything I've down-played it and the name of the individual has been changed. However it was not to be glossed over. It really was my only down side within those first seven months.

If that particular individual should read this and recognise himself... well mate as they say, you reap what you sow. I will say however that following a further far more serious incident in his future his attitude did change for the better.

I have changed a few names, and in places, such as our visit to the Eros centre I've used initials to avoid me getting a law suit or a contract on my head.

Many lads who I'm still in touch with I asked if they objected to being included by name.

Those men I've named and wasn't able to track down for permission, I can only say 'I hope you've no objection and I've written nothing for you to be ashamed of or embarrassed about. In fact I hope if you ever read the book you'll enjoy it and it'll bring back some good memories.

I apologise for the quality of the photos – in short they are old and even enhancement hasn't been able to perk them up.

My assessment of how some married personnel would have behaved if the shit really did hit the fan is not meant offensively. It would have been a more than understandable reaction to worry about your family and ensure their safety before running off to the front. However what I have written is factual; I did hear this subject discussed in conversation on more than one occasion.

Now the Thank you's...

They are numerous and heartfelt. A great deal of ex-Sixteeners have contributed to this book with stories recollections and photos. Michael Evens for allowing me to use his photo of the main gate and 23 Engineer cookhouse in the snow, this was just how the entrance looked on my first morning. Tim Marshall for the bar photos showing a few of the great wall paintings; I never ever thought we'd see these again and they need to be recorded in print, plus his other various photos; thanks Tim.

Steve 'Doogle' Adkins, Stephen Hannon, Baz Gazey, Frank Butler, for their amazing recollection of the Scratch and Eros centre, plus other memory joggers. Chris 'Benny' Dearne for the New Year's Eve bar story.

Paul, Gary and Robert regarding the forces papers; Russ 'Benny' Bennett my section oppo and Doogle again, for the reminders regarding our search course.

Input by Alec McCrystal, Tom Byrne and others.

The photo of the Winkle, had to be included, the pub was a part of Royal Engineers Osnabruck legend; I don't know where I got it or who took it, but thanks to the owner whoever he is.

Also a big thanks to those who proof read for me and your feedback.

It is inevitably, that a few, and I hope it will only be a few, will read this memoir and disagree with some of the content or timings. My reply to this is the same as the comment I wrote at the end of 'Boys to Men', that I worked hard to ensure accuracy.

I still have reference material from the time and old comrades with whom I double checked. 1974 was a long time ago for all of us; if you see me at Sapperfest we'll discuss it over a beer.

So to round it up... 16 Field Squadron RE is off to Ballykelly, County Londonderry to carry out a four month tour of duty in an Engineer and Search Team role; I better get scribbling.

Manufactured by Amazon.ca
Bolton, ON

27321857R00120